The 21st-Century Elementary School Library Program

The 21st-Century Elementary School Library Program

Managing for Results

Second Edition

Carl A. Harvey II

LIBRARIES UNLIMITED™

An Imprint of ABC-CLIO, LLC

Santa Barbara, California • Denver, Colorado

Library of Congress Cataloguing-in-Publication Data
Names: Harvey, Carl A., II, author.
Title: The 21st-century elementary school library program : managing for results /
  Carl A. Harvey II.
Other titles: 21st century elementary library media program | Twenty-first century
  elementary school library program
Description: Second edition. | Santa Barbara, California : Libraries Unlimited, an imprint
  of ABC-CLIO, LLC, [2017] | Includes bibliographical references and index.
Identifiers: LCCN 2016029844 (print) | LCCN 2016048549 (ebook) | ISBN 9781440842443
  (paperback : acid-free paper) | ISBN 9781440842450 (ebook)
Subjects: LCSH: Elementary school libraries—United States—Administration. | Instructional
  materials centers—United States—Administration.
Classification: LCC Z675.S3 H2687 2017 (print) | LCC Z675.S3 (ebook) | DDC 027.8/2220973—dc23
LC record available at https://lccn.loc.gov/2016029844

ISBN: 978-1-4408-4244-3
EISBN: 978-1-4408-4245-0

21 20 19 18 17   1 2 3 4 5

This book is also available as an eBook.

Libraries Unlimited
An Imprint of ABC-CLIO, LLC

ABC-CLIO, LLC
130 Cremona Drive, P.O. Box 1911
Santa Barbara, California 93116–1911
www.abc-clio.com

This book is printed on acid-free paper ∞

Manufactured in the United States of America

Thanks, as always, to my amazing family—especially my adorable nieces and nephews—Matthew, Hannah, Savannah, Lilli, Luke, and Emma. I love you all.

Thanks to my ABC-CLIO family—Becky, Kathryn, Sharon, Marlene, and many more too numerous to mention for all their guidance and support and encouragement throughout my career.

Thanks to my Longwood family—I've already learned so much from Audrey, Frances, and Karla. I so appreciate their support and help as I transition to the next chapter in my career.

Finally, this book (just as the first edition) is dedicated to the students and faculty at North Elementary School (2002–2015) and Lowell Elementary School (1998–2002). Without teachers willing to collaboratively plan, teach, and assess; without administrators who support and encourage; without students who love their school library; and without parents who support the program, we would not have been able to create successful school library programs! I am so grateful for everything I learned from my time at these amazing schools! It truly is a gift I will forever hold in my heart!

Contents

Figures

About the Author

Carl A. Harvey II is an instructor of school librarianship at Longwood University in Farmville, Virginia. Previously, he was an elementary school librarian in Indiana for 17 years. He was the 2011–2012 president of the American Association of School Librarians (AASL). In AASL, he has also served as chair of the Affiliate Assembly, co-chair for the 2007 National Conference in Reno, Nevada, and a Member-at-Large on the AASL Board of Directors. He was a member of the Association for Library Services to Children (ALSC) 2014 Caldecott Metal Committee. He is also a past-president of the Association for Indiana Media Educators (AIME) and the Indiana Library Federation (ILF). He is a member of Virginia Association of School Librarians, International Society for Technology in Education, and the International Literacy Association.

He is coeditor for *School Library Connection*—a professional development platform published by ABC-CLIO. He has published several articles in various professional journals, including *School Library Journal, School Library Connection, Library Media Connection, School Library Monthly*, and *Teacher-Librarian*. He has written five books—*The LMS in the Writing Process* (coauthored with Marge Cox and Susan Page) (2007); *No School Library Left Behind: Leadership, School Improvement, and the Media Specialist* (2008); *The 21st Century Elementary School Library Media Program* (2010); *Adult Learners: School Librarians and Professional Development* (2012); *Leading the Common Core Initiative: A Guide for K-6 Librarians* (coauthored with Linda Mills) (2015)—published by ABC-CLIO. Carl has also presented at numerous state and national conferences.

Some of his awards include Outstanding New Library Media Specialist (1999), Outstanding Media Specialist (2007), and the Peggy L. Pfeiffer Service Award (2007) all from the Association for Indiana Media Educators. The library program at North Elementary School has been recognized with the Blue Ribbon for Exemplary School Media Programs by the Association for Indiana Media Educators (2005) and the National School Library Media Program of the Year Award (2007) from the American Association of School Librarians.

He has served on advisory boards for several different vendors as well as part of the committee that revised the Library Media Standards for the National Board for Professional Teaching Standards in 2010. Carl also consults part time for C.L.A.S.S. (Connected Learning Assures Successful Students) in Indianapolis, Indiana.

Introduction

Reading through the first edition of this book, I asked myself, "Is it really time to revise this book?" While I believe there is relevant and helpful bits of information in the first edition, I also looked at all the things that have grown and expanded since then—eBooks, makerspaces, technology, Common Core, Learning Commons, ESSA, and so much more. What I have always loved about school libraries is they are a place of evolution and change. No two days are ever the same, so there are always new ideas, new ways to look at an issue, and new ways for the program to grow. Of course, you also think about all the things you wished you had said or included. So, armed with all this, I marched forward answering the question with a resounding YES!

As much as some things change, some remains the same. Excitement and opportunities still abound for today's school library programs. The rapid expansion of information available in a multitude of formats has created not only an abundance of resources but also the need for skills to find, evaluate, and use that information effectively. The explosion of online tools and resources has increased the ability for students to be a part of creating and disseminating new information. School library programs are even more a critical link to preparing students for their future.

In 2007, the American Association of School Librarians released the *Standards for the 21st Century Learner*. This document painted a picture of the skills students need to be successful. Library instruction has focused on inquiry and helping guide students to find, evaluate, and use information accurately and effectively. Nine years later, AASL is working on updating its standards with a release date of November 2017. While it is still too soon to know what the revision will look like, it is pretty safe to say it will continue to help move our field forward.

The economic and educational climate of the last few years has not looked fondly at school libraries. Positions have been lost and budgets have been cut all over the country. Librarians can spend time wallowing in what they don't have and what they've lost, or librarians can focus on rebuilding, expanding the potential of school libraries, and making sure that everyone knows the role and value of a school library program in a successful school. There are pockets of common sense prevailing and positions have been returning in spots. My hope is this book gives some ideas and strategies for creating dynamic programs that no one would ever want to be without in their school.

In the pages that follow, there are a plethora of ideas and strategies for creating, implementing, and managing an elementary school library. Keeping up and harnessing the best of all that information and tools for student learning will be the job of the 21st-century school librarian!

In Chapter 1, the focus is on the role of the school library program in the past, the present, and the future. In order to create a vision for the future, we have to know from where we came. The role school library program has played in schools has been changing and evolving for years. How does the 21st-century environment continue to change that role? Chapter 2 focuses on the people school librarians work with every day. How does the school librarian work with various stakeholders? Why are they important? What opportunities for partnership and collaboration are available? Chapter 3 focuses on communication. School librarians must be effective communicators so that stakeholders know what they do, how and why they do it, how they can help, and why the media specialist's role in the school is so vital.

Chapter 4 focuses on curriculum. The heart of the school library program is the connection made between 21st-century standards and the classroom curriculum. How do school librarian and teachers collaborate? How does the school librarian make those connections with teachers? What role does the school librarian play in assessment? Chapter 5 is all about the programming offered to students. Beyond instruction, what kind of programming should the school librarian create to promote reading, provide enrichments programs, and host celebrations? What events bring people into the school library? Chapter 6 focuses on technology. How does technology impact the school library? While a separate chapter focuses on technology, technology is embedded into all the chapters because that is the reality of the 21st century.

Chapter 7 looks at library administration. Behind-the-scenes jobs have to be done to make the school library program function effectively. How can some of the new web tools make the school librarian's job easier? Chapter 8 is a new chapter that is reorganization and expansion of content from other chapters about the evaluation of school library programs and personnel. Chapter 9 examines budgets. Money certainly doesn't grow on trees, so how does the school librarian find money to support the program? What are some alternatives to funding provided by the school? Chapter 10 discusses about library collections and the influx of formats of materials. How do 21st-century students' needs and interests change, what school libraries collections look like? How does technology impact the collection? What role will eBooks play in elementary libraries?

The book concludes with two more chapters. Chapter 11 focuses on advocacy. It is important for the school librarian to get past being the sole advocate for the school library program. How does the school librarian motivate and enlist others to go and be the voice for the program? While it may be the last chapter, it may very well be the most important. Chapter 12 is all about the school librarian's role as a leader. There is no doubt that successful school librarians are leaders in their schools? Why is that important? How does being involved beyond the school library help promote the school library program? All of these issues have been organized into separate chapters in order to make it easier to find specific elements, but we know that school librarians do all of these interconnected things to create, grow, and maintain a school library program.

Today's school librarian should never be content with the status quo but rather constantly looking for opportunities and experiences that will take the school library program to the next level. This book is a prime example of constantly looking at how elementary school libraries can improve. Whether just starting out in the school library or a seasoned veteran, the key is to look ahead so that the school library program evolves as the needs of the students and staff evolves. One thing that hasn't changed is that school library programs of the future will continue to develop and foster a culture of lifelong learning for everyone.

CHAPTER 1

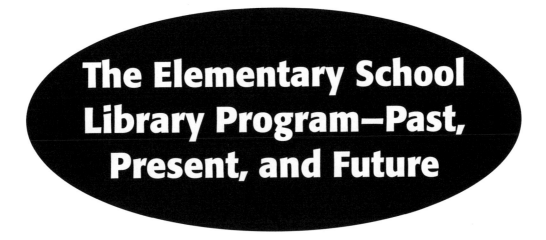

The Elementary School Library Program—Past, Present, and Future

As good as we are, we can always get better.

> —Barbara Pedersen, president and founder, C.L.A.S.S.
> (Connected Learning Assures Successful Students)

In every workshop she gives, every meeting she runs, every aspect of the business she operates, and in every classroom she works in, Barbara shares her vision for moving forward. It has become a personal mantra for many. What a powerful message to celebrate the current realities, but at the same time focus thoughts on what can be done next to make it even better! Most of this book was built on that mantra. The constant focus on what the school librarian is doing and how the school librarian can make it even better is a perfect picture of how school library programs should look out into the future.

Elementary school library programs have certainly evolved over the years. From nonexistent to a place where students checked out resources, to a place where students are finding, evaluating, using, and creating information, elementary school library programs have continued to evolve and grow. Programs will continue to alter in the 21st century. As the needs of students and learning environments change, so will the school library program.

The Past

The history of elementary school libraries is brief. Libraries in schools were just beginning as the 20th century began. Most of those libraries were also in secondary schools. The following timeline lists some of the major events in the history of elementary school libraries and how they have changed over the years.

Mid-1800s to 1900	Schools were beginning to put collections together in libraries in the late 1800s. The first school librarians were hired right around the turn of the century. Most of these libraries and librarians were at secondary level schools. (Woolls 2014, p. 4)
1896	National Education Association (NEA) creates a School Library Section. (Morris 2004, p. 4)
1914	American Library Association (ALA) creates a School Library Section. (Morris 2004, p. 4)
1920	The first school library standards are published by ALA. *Standard Library Organization and Equipment for Secondary Schools* written by a committee under the chairmanship of Charles C. Certain. While these standards did not mention or apply to elementary school, the conversation began about what school libraries in the United States should look like. (Morris 2004, p. 7)
1925	The ALA and the NEA publish the first standards for elementary school libraries—also chaired by Charles C. Certain. However, not many elementary schools had libraries and the books that were published were often part of collections in the classroom. (Woolls 2014, p. 5; Morris 2004, p. 8)
1945	*School Libraries for Today and Tomorrow* is published by the American Association of School Librarians (AASL). These standards painted a picture of the different roles between public librarians and school librarians. Frances Henne, a member of the committee who wrote the 1945 standards, advocated for collaboration between school librarians and classroom teachers. (Kester 2004, p. 954)
1951	The AASL is formed as a division of ALA.
1960	*Standards for School Library Programs* is published by the AASL. Nineteen other professional organizations cooperated on this project. These standards highlighted the school librarian's role as a teacher and began to articulate the incorporation of audio–visual materials in school libraries. (Kester 2004, p. 956)
1964	U.S. Office of Education report by Mary Helen Mahar and Doris C. Holladay said that fewer than 50 percent of elementary schools had libraries. (Woolls 2014, p. 6)
1965	Elementary and Secondary Education Act (ESEA) is passed including funds specifically to purchase school library materials (Title II).
1969	The AASL and the NEA's Department of Audiovisual Instruction (DAVI) publish *Standards for School Media Programs*. These guide-

lines provided detailed quantitative guidelines for school libraries. (Kester 2004, p. 958)

1975	The AASL and the Association for Educational Communications and Technology (formerly DAVI) publish *Media Programs: District and School* (Kester 2004, p. 959). These standards placed a great emphasis on the instructional role of the school librarian and not just a support program.
1979	The first White House Conference on Library and Information Science is held in Washington, DC. They made 64 recommendations including a guarantee of media services in each public school. Unfortunately cuts in government spending in the 1980s delayed their implementation. (Morris 2004, p. 15)
1980s	Funding requirements are rewritten and school libraries are required to compete for funds both at the federal and the state levels. Changes in certification have been altered so that in some places a certified school librarian is not required in the school library. (Woolls 2014, p. 6)
1988	*Information Power* is published jointly by the AASL and the Association for Educational Communications and Technology. The new standards focus on the role of the school librarian as a teacher, information specialist, and instructional consultant.
1998	*Information Power: Building Partnerships for Learning* is published by the AASL and the Association for Educational Communications and Technology. This document added program administrator and instructional partners to the role of the school librarian. They also included the Information Literacy Standards for Student Learning.
2002	First Lady Laura Bush hosts the White House Conference on School Libraries on June 4, 2002. In her opening remarks, Mrs. Bush said, "Libraries allow children to ask questions about the world and find the answers. And the wonderful thing is that once a child learns to use a library, the doors to learning are always open." Many current leaders, such as Dr. Gary Hartzell and Dr. Keith Curry Lance spoke at the conference and shared the importance of school libraries in today's schools. (Morris 2004, pp. 18–19)
2007	The AASL releases the *Standards for 21st Century Learner*: www. ala.org/ala/mgrps/divs/aasl/guidelinesandstandards/ learningstandards/standards.cfm. The standards focus on inquiry, social learning, ethical skills, and are designed to provide a framework of skills students will need for the future. School librarians will take these to work with classroom teacher as they combine them with content area standards to design lessons and units.

2007	At the same time, the International Society for Technology in Education releases its refresh of the National Educational Technology Standards. The original NETs focused on the technology tools that students needed to learn, but the revised version centers on the skills they will need to live in a digital society.
2009	The AASL releases *The Standards for the 21st Century Learner in Action.* This new document took the standards and provided examples and benchmarks at various levels along with potential assessment options. It helped to paint a picture for what the new standards looked like at elementary, middle, and high school.
2009	The AASL releases the long-awaited guidelines that would replace *Information Power 2.* The new guidelines are titled *Empowering Learners: Guidelines for School Library Program*: www.ala.org/ ala/mgrps/divs/aasl/guidelinesandstandards/learningstandards/ guidelines.cfm. The new document divides the guidelines into three sections—teaching for learning, building the learning environment, and empowering learning through leadership.
2011–2012	The AASL gives a congressional briefing in Washington, DC, outlining the role and responsibilities of the 21st-century school library program and librarian. Over 28,000 supporters of school libraries sign the White House petition. The petition crossed the threshold required to receive a response from the White House.
2016	Every Student Succeed Act (ESSA) is signed into law. This new law, which replaces the 2007 No Child Left Behind Act, has specific language about effective school librarians and sources of potential federal funds to support them. Much work is still needed to understand and obtain this funding, but this is a major start in the right direction.

The Present

The present status of school libraries varies greatly. From districts with no librarians to states that require one in every school, the amount of support for school libraries is different all over the country. Take a look in the further readings for the most updated information about the requirements for becoming a school librarian in today's universities and the requirements from each state. Budgets for collections vary greatly. School librarians all over the country are painting a picture of what today's school library program should be for students. When the economy took a hit, so did school libraries. However, now there are pockets of places where positions are returning. There is still much work to do to achieve a goal of a school librarian for every school, but work continues every day toward that goal. The school librarians of today being transformational in how their school library programs impact student learning will largely shape the future.

The Future

Looking to the future, in 2017, the AASL will release a revised document of standards and guidelines. These updated and/or revised documents from the 2007 standards will chart a course for the profession for the next 10 years. This is an exciting time to be a school librarian. There is a great potential in what the future holds. School librarians have to be ready to take that opportunity and lead! Building on the past, learning from the adventures, and charting a course for the future, the key is school librarians being at the forefront of creating and implementing the future.

The Vision

A key thing to keep in mind is that these documents and standards referred to in the past as well as in the present and future paint the outline and give the big picture of what an effective and quality school library program looks like. The real power in an effective school library program is the role the school librarian and all other stakeholders take to add the color, shading, and detail to the program. School librarians need to be able to clearly articulate what the program is doing and where the program needs to go. Using these standards, bringing in stakeholders, and creating a culture of possibilities, the school librarian can build and implement a shared vision for quality school library program in their school.

Works Cited

American Association of School Librarians. *Standards for the 21st Century Learner.* Chicago, IL: American Association of School Librarians, 2007.

American Association of School Librarians. *Empowering Learners: Guidelines for School Library Programs.* Chicago, IL: American Association of School Librarians, 2009.

American Association of School Librarians. *Standards for the 21st Century Learner in Action.* Chicago, IL: American Association of School Librarians, 2009.

Bush, Laura. "Opening Remarks." White House Conference on School Libraries. White House, Washington, DC. June 4, 2002. Accessed January 18, 2009. www.white house.gov/news/releases/2002/06/20020604–12.html.

International Society for Technology in Education. *National Educational Technology Standards for Students*, 2nd edition. Eugene, OR: International Society for Technology in Education, 2007.

Kester, Diane D., and Plummer Alton Jones. "Frances Henne and the Development of School Library Standards." *Library Trends* 52 (Spring 2004): 952–962.

Morris, Betty J. *Administering the School Library Media Center*, 4th edition. Westport, CT: Libraries Unlimited, 2004.

Pedersen, Barbara. "Personal Quote." E-mail to the author. March 2, 2009.

Woolls, Blanche. *The School Library Manager*, 5th edition. Santa Barbara, CA: Libraries Unlimited, 2014.

Further Reading

Adcock, Donald, and Susan Ballard. "65 Still the One." *Knowledge Quest* 43, no. 4 (2015): 8–15.

American Association of School Librarians. *Library Education & Licensing*. Accessed May 22, 2016. http://www.ala.org/aasl/education/recruitment/licensing.

Barnett, Cassandra. "The More Things Change the More They Stay the Same." *Knowledge Quest* 43, no. 4 (2015): 30–38.

Smith-Faulkner, Renee. "Creating a Transformative Library Vision." *Texas Library Journal* 91, no. 4 (2015): 6–7.

CHAPTER 2

Influence is derived from the perceptions of the person to be influenced, not from the perceptions of the person doing the influencing. The key to building influence lies in your ability to shape the perceptions of others.

— Dr. Gary Hartzell, *Building Influence for the School Librarian: Tenets, Targets, and Tactics*

The biggest part of the school librarian's job is working with people—teachers, students, parents, principals, school boards, community members, volunteers, and other school librarians. All of these groups have a very important impact on the school librarians and school library programs, but at a variety of different levels. Hartzell divides these up into two levels—Level 1 contains administrators, principals, and school board members, and Level 2 contains students, parents, and community members (Hartzell 2003, p. 91). Level 1 has direct control over the resources needed. Level 2 does not, but can be important because the ability to influence that group can impact and encourage the decision made by Level 1. Determining the needs of each group gives the school librarian the opportunity to not only meet those needs but to also exceed them.

Another way to think about it is the spheres of influence. There are not many positions in a school building that have the unique perspective of school librarians. Not only do school librarians teach every student, but they also work with every staff member. School librarians build relationships with parents and community leaders to support the role school librarians play in the school ecosystem and to help fund the materials and resources the students need. School librarians have to be active and involved in working with all of these different groups in the spheres of influence. (See Figure 2.1, Spheres of Influences.)

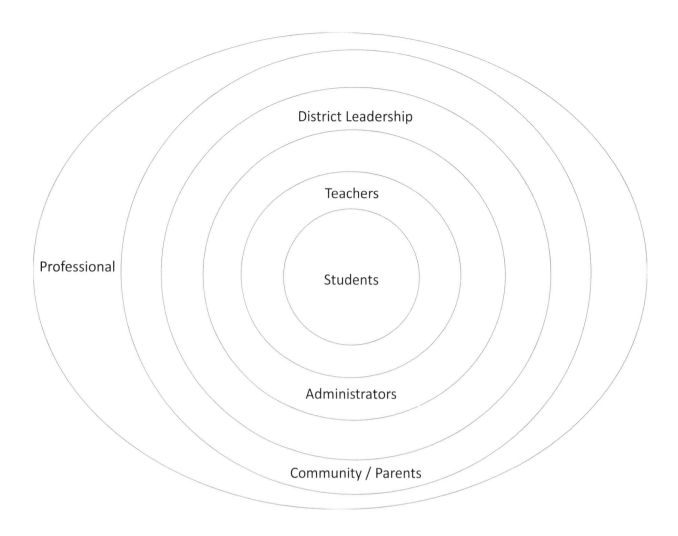

Figure 2.1 Spheres of Influences.

Each group has a perception of the school librarian (and depending on their past experiences with school librarians it can be either good or bad); therefore, it is important that school librarians make sure they have the right perception of what a school librarian should be doing in today's schools. When starting out as a school librarian or even just switching to a new school, one of the very first things a school librarian must do is build relationships in all those spheres. Everything in the school library program is dependent on the relationships built with stakeholders, so the key is to build those bridges in the beginning. Often it is easy to get caught up in "fixing" things in the school library (the fiction section needs to be shifted, the nonfiction collection needs to be weeded, or work on spending the budget), but those things can wait. The most important element in building a strong and solid school library program is to build a good and strong working relationship!

The School Librarian Works With Principals

Most administrators learn about school library programs from only one source—school librarians! They know about the experiences they had as a child in school, as a teacher in a school, and now as an administrator in a school. Take advantage of that opportunity to help guide them on their journey about learning the value, potential, and power of the school library program. (See Figure 2.2, What Should an Administrator Expect of a School Librarian?)

Building a working relationship with an administrator is not an easy task. While school librarians are totally focused on the program and how that impacts the school, to the principal the school library is just a part of the entire school he or she is trying to manage. The school librarian's job in building relationships is to take the initiative to see how the school library program can help the principal achieve his or her goals for the entire school.

For example, one librarian was working with a new principal. The principal shared that he was using a theme of professional development dealing with building bridges. So, the librarian took the initiative to pull all the resources—both print and nonprint available in the library—about bridges and shared them with the principal. The administrator instantly knew there was support for him in the school librarian. It is sometimes these simple gestures that can lead to amazing opportunities.

Chapter 3 focuses on communication and various vehicles a school librarian can use to share his or her message. Often, the method and the phrasing of things can also be important. Consider the following statements. The original one is typical of what an administrator might hear from a school librarian. The revised is a possible better slant on the same issue. However, phrasing is the key.

✦ *Original:* My budget is inadequate.
  ✧ *Revised:* With the new initiative for math, I've been reviewing the math collection. Most of the titles are out of date. The average copyright date is 1976. To support the projects, teachers are assigning and provide the resources students need to succeed, additional funds are needed.

A school librarian teaches.   They work with students in the school library and all over the building to become information literate.

A school librarian collaborates.   They work with teachers to plan, instruct, and evaluate student learning. They work with administrators to implement building-wide initiatives and the school improvement plan.

A school librarian provides.   The school librarian builds a collection of resources—print, nonprint, and digital—that provide students and staff with the information they need to be successful.

A school librarian communicates.   A school librarian talks, e-mails, tweets, blogs, and shares with administrators, teachers, students, parents, and community members about how the school library program directly relates to the vision of the school.

A school librarian leads.   Administrators and teachers see the school librarian as a leader. They are active on school committees, contribute to building initiatives, and are respected for their thoughts and ideas.

A school librarian looks forward.   They craft a vision for the school library program, and how it can be a powerful tool in helping the school reach its goal. The school librarian is always thinking about the future.

A school librarian shares.   They design and present professional development for faculty and staff that supports the school improvement plan.

A school librarian innovates.   They are willing to try new things. They are looking for new ways to get even better. They are creative to work around obstacles.

A school librarian sees the world.   They work with everyone in the school, so they have a global perspective of the school environment.

A school librarian learns.   They love to keep learning about new ideas and strategies for working with students and teachers. They want to be lifelong learners just like they hope their students will be.

A school librarian integrates.   They are a leader in using technology in their instruction. They share their knowledge about books and authors. They work to embed these resources into instruction.

But most of all, the school librarian does not work alone.   For a school to have a successful school library program, it takes everyone (the school librarian, teacher, administrators, and the library staff) working together for the benefit of the students.

Figure 2.2   What Should an Administrator Expect of a School Librarian?

✦ *Original:* My technology is all out of date.

    ✧ *Revised:* Yesterday two classes were in the school library working on research, but the computers wouldn't connect to the databases because they were too slow. It wasted an hour of instructional time for that class. Do you think we could write a grant to update our computers?

✦ *Original:* My support staff is insufficient. I don't have any time for the administrative functions of the library.

    ✧ *Revised:* During the last three weeks, I have been booked solid with classes. At the same time, a tremendous amount of books circulated from the library, and the new books that I selected and ordered are still sitting in the boxes. How can teaching and learning be the focus but at the same time allow time to complete these clerical jobs? The overflowing cart of books is an example that no one has had any time to shelve them so students can read them again. Could you help me find some volunteers for the library?

The original statements contained the same information as the revised statements, but the difference is the revised statements connected it directly to student learning and achievement. The second set of statements contained data as well to support the argument. This does not mean that changing the phrases will automatically change the answer a school librarian might receive from an administrator. However, it may just leave a seed planted in the administrator's mind if additional resources do become available.

School librarian and administrators have more in common than one might think.

✦ The principal and school librarian work with every staff member.

✦ The principal and school librarian interact with all students.

✦ The principal and school librarian need to be curriculum leaders in the school.

✦ The principal and school librarian have administrative roles, such as dealing with budgets, facilities, and so forth.

✦ The principal and school librarian have a global perspective being able to see the "big picture" of what is happening in the school.

✦ The principal and school librarian (especially likely in an elementary school) have a job where they are the only one in their building.

Use these similarities as the springboard for building a relationship with the principal. The similarities can lead to the opportunity for the two to share in conversations that no one else in the building could have. Many administrators come to rely on their school librarian because they can talk about school improvement, issues in the building with them because the school librarian unlike a teacher can see beyond his or her classroom or grade level. School librarians will find that they build influence by connecting these similarities between the principal and the school librarian roles in the school (Hartzell 2003, p. 31). However, the school librarian has to take the lead in building the relationship and demonstrate to the administrator the common bonds between their two roles.

An administrator is just another patron in the school library, but just like all the other groups their needs are different. They are looking for ways to move the school forward. How do they improve student achievement? How do they provide professional development? How do they implement instructional strategies? The school librarians should be following what the administrator is thinking and doing. Just as with other patrons, providing them with resources, ideas, and support will garner a positive reaction.

Consider the principal who is implementing a new instructional model for the school. Should the school librarian look for ways to implement that in his or her instruction? Yes! During collaborative planning sessions, could the school librarian suggest ways teacher could implement the new model? Yes! Could the school librarian provide training and ideas, such as how to use technology with the new model? Yes! Administrators will notice what is happening, but use some of the communication tools discussed in Chapter 3 to make sure to tell them what is going on, too.

Words only go so far. Actions speak louder. Look for ways to demonstrate the program you want to achieve. Invite them down for lessons and programs. Demonstrate for them how what is happening in the school library impacts student achievement. Follow up with an e-mail thanking them for visiting and providing the administrator with ideas on how to continue to push to the next level.

The school librarian does not always know what kind of experience the administrator has had with school library programs in the past. The school librarian needs to be intentional with what he or she does, says, and writes to help paint the picture of what the 21st-century school library program looks like and why it is a critical element for student success.

Teachers

The school librarian has a unique role in the school because they have the opportunity to work with every teacher in the building. This potential for impact is huge.

Teachers are half of the equation to collaboration and instruction in the school library. They bring with them the content standards, and school librarians bring information skills and inquiry process. Marrying the two together provides for quality learning opportunities for students. (See Figure 2.3, What Should a Teacher Expect of a School Librarian?)

Students are assigned a teacher for an entire year in elementary school; so to reach the students, the school librarian has to connect with the teacher. Elementary teachers can be very possessive of their students. Often the school librarian must work to develop a level of trust. Teachers have to believe that the school librarian can teach their students just as effectively as they can. This trust takes time to develop. The school librarian must remain patient, persistent, and follow-through when making promises in order to begin to establish that trust.

When collaborating with teachers, school librarians usually need a thick skin. Don't take it personally if teachers don't jump up and down with excitement over a proposed project or lesson. Keep throwing out the ideas and suggestions, and eventually one will connect. Persistence is important. Be aware of the standards they need to cover. Be aware of students' deficiencies

A school librarian teaches.   They work with students in the school library and all over the building to become information literate.

A school librarian collaborates.   They work with teachers to plan, instruct, and evaluate student learning. They work with administrators to implement building-wide initiatives and the school improvement plan.

A school librarian provides.   The school librarian builds a collection of resources—print, nonprint, and digital—that provide students and staff with the information they need to be successful.

A school librarian reads.   They enjoy sharing great books with students and teachers. They help entice students to have a lifetime love of reading. They have ideas on incorporating great books into a variety of curriculum topics. Share with them the great books you find, too.

A school librarian communicates.   A school librarian talks, e-mails, tweets, blogs, and shares with administrators, teachers, students, parents, and community members about how the school library program directly relates to the vision of the school.

A school librarian leads.   Administrators and teachers see the school librarian as a leader. They are active on school committees, contribute to building initiatives, and are respected for their thoughts and ideas.

A school librarian looks forward.   They craft a vision for the school library program, and how it can be a powerful tool in helping the school reach its goal. The school librarian is always thinking about the future.

A school librarian shares.   They design and present professional development for faculty and staff that supports the school improvement plan.

A school librarian innovates.   They are willing to try new things. They are looking for new ways to get even better. They are creative to work around obstacles.

A school librarian helps.   They are always willing to help out when needed even when it is not their "job." Ask for their help when needed. It makes them happy to be of service.

A school librarian learns.   They love to keep learning about new ideas and strategies for working with students and teachers. They want to be lifelong learners just like they hope their students will be.

A school librarian integrates.   They are a leader in using technology in their instruction. They share their knowledge about books and authors. They work to embed these resources into instruction.

But most of all, the school librarian does not work alone.   For a school to have a successful school library program it takes everyone (the school librarian, teachers, administration, and the school library staff) working together for the benefit of the students.

Figure 2.3   What Should a Teacher Expect of a School Librarian?

on the standardized tests. Be aware of the themes and units they study. Use that knowledge to help better define a rationale for working with the teachers.

Often school librarians might hear the phrase "work with the living" when looking for collaborative partners. This is a good place to start, but those kids in a "nonliving teacher's" room also need learning opportunities. School librarians must continue to work toward breaking down those barriers, so they work with all the teachers (and therefore students) in the building.

Ideas to break down those barriers include:

✦ Connect with the teacher's interest or passion. What kind of resources, projects, or ideas can the school librarian suggest that will be a part of or enhance student learning?

✦ Connect with the content the teacher dislikes. If there is a part of the curriculum he or she doesn't like teaching, this could be a perfect opportunity to suggest collaborating together. The teacher gets through something he or she dislikes teaching and the students get a worthwhile learning experience.

✦ Be aware of standardized testing results. Which areas did the students in the building score low? How could the school library program offer a project or activity that might help students improve in that area? Use that as an opening when trying to work with teachers.

✦ During staff meetings, professional development meeting, or anything related to working with staff members, model using the tools and resources that would be possible to use with students. Suggest that just as the school librarian is helping the faculty, they would be glad to use these same activities and resources with students as well.

Often school librarians are frustrated when teachers refuse to work with them. The job requires a certain level of persistence and knack for seizing opportunities at just the right time.

The best way to build a relationship with a teacher is delivery on promises made. Follow through is key. This continues to build the level of trust. As teachers know the school librarian is going to follow through on whatever they promise, the teachers are going to begin to develop that trust for more involved projects and activities. The amount of time it takes varies from teacher to teacher. But, the key is the school librarian doesn't give up but keeps persevering.

School librarians also have to be where the teachers are! Waiting for teachers to come to the library could be a lonely wait—especially if the teachers are not used to someone dynamic in that role. Go to where the teachers are! Eat lunch in the lunchroom and vary the time as much as possible to eat with different grade levels. Attend grade-level planning meetings. Participate in social events and on school-wide committees. Just positively interacting with teachers every day helps in building relationships that can eventually lead to instructional collaborations!

While the first connections are likely made with classroom teachers, it is also important to reach out to related arts teachers (art, music, physical education); special education teachers; literacy coaches; and the school counselor. All of these folks teach kids, too, so it is important to look for the collaborative potential with every teacher in the building.

School Boards

Every year during National School Library Month, a district library coordinator sends a package updating the school board about the role school libraries played in the district. Another school librarian makes sure that for every literacy event, such as the annual author visit, that an invitation is always sent to each of the school board members. Still another school librarian has annual reading days where she invites the community—including school board members—to the school library to read stories with students. A great way for school board members to learn what is happening in the school library is by bringing them in to see it.

Working with school boards directly will require some preplanning on behalf of the school librarian. Any communication with the school board should go through the superintendent to ensure the proper chain of command. Consider an invitation to tour the school library or the school librarian could make a presentation to the school board highlighting the role he or she plays in the school. If the official channels are not an option, there are other ways school board members can learn about the program. Invite the local newspaper or media at a program or project for a positive story. School members will take notice. Before contacting the media, make sure to follow any district guidelines.

In one district, once a year at a school board meeting, the librarians work to present about what the school library program is doing in the district, and how it impacts student learning. This is a group of individuals who often have huge impact on staffing, budgets, and other impactful decisions. It is important that they have a clear vision of why school libraries and school librarians are essential. Building that relationship can be most helpful should there ever be any question regarding the importance of school libraries.

Students

At the heart of the school library programs are the #1 patrons—students. During the five to seven years they are in elementary school (depending on grade configurations), the school librarian is one of the few teachers who they will work with every year. They should feel comfortable asking for help. They should feel comfortable coming to the school library. Students should feel like this is "our" school library with everyone who uses it having ownership of the facility and program. Consider the student who every time came to the library the first place he headed was the school librarian's office. The student knew if he needed help finding a book, or had a question, or just need a quieter place for a moment, he was always welcome to visit the school librarian.

There are a couple of ways that school librarians get the opportunity to connect with students. The first is during instruction. Whether this is in a collaborative planned environment or whether it is during a "specials" time when the school librarian is covering prep time, either way provides the chance for the school librarian to work with students. Schedule will be covered more in depth in Chapter 7. Another way is by creating an environment where students enjoy coming to the school library during recess or other free time to read and explore.

Consider the reference interview. The first part of that equation is that the person needing information has to feel comfortable and should be willing to go to the school librarian and ask questions. The same can be said for elementary students. They have to feel comfortable that the school librarian is there to help them. Attitudes are important. Students need to feel they have the support to help guide them to where they can find the answer.

Library collections in schools are focused heavily on curriculum, but at the same time also contain resources for general student interests. Students love coming to the library to learn and explore. Consider a school where there are puppets available for students to create their own shows. One school even goes so far as to purchase book characters that students can check out with the matching book. Another school has a writing center setup with paper, crayons, and pencils that students can use to create their own writing adventures. Another school library has a math center filled with games, problem-solving resources, and other math-related topics. Students know anytime they are in the school library, they can use any of these things. The climate is such that students feel free to explore and learn. These stations may even evolve into creating a Makerspace in the library.

The school library space is one that belongs to everyone. Students should not only feel a sense of being welcomed but also that is a place they belong. They will have great ideas to make the library even better, so make sure to take time to ask them their thoughts. Chapter 10 discusses more about advisory committees and ways to gather input from stakeholders.

Parents

Some parents' only interactions with the school library program are when they hear about lost or overdue books. Look for ways to keep parents informed of what happens in the school library beyond just those notices. Give them the opportunity to see the positive things happening in the school library. Write pieces for the school newsletter. Consider sending home a school library newsletter periodically. Instead of using paper, use e-mail or post it on the school webpage. How about setting up a school library blog to showcase what is happening in the school library? How about a Twitter account for the library? How about a Facebook page for parents to follow? Can you utilize the school library website to share what is happening for parents? Can you embed widgets of some of these tools on the school library website? These technology options could serve two purposes because it would also serve as a way to communicate to students, teachers, and administrators. When working on projects that require students to spend time on them at home, send home a list of resources students can access from the school library website.

Parent Volunteers

They can be invaluable to helping return materials back to the shelves, processing new materials, running book fairs, and so forth. At the same time, this gives them a prime view of what is happening in the school library. They can see the classes and projects. They can see the benefits the program has for their child(ren).

PTA/PTO groups are another great way to share what is happening in the school library. Attend these meetings and talk about the school library program. Consider ways that the school librarian can support them. How about offering to update their webpage? How about volunteering to help them with arranging and scheduling enrichment programs? Support the special events they have in the school by attending. Be a visual presence! Thank them for supporting the school library. They often want to support things that will impact the entire school—the school library program is a perfect place! The school librarian's active involvement can often lead to financial benefits for the school library program.

Community Members

One of the major connections with the community is the partnership one can build with local business. Whenever possible, the school librarian should look for ways to connect with local businesses. For example, ask an independent bookstore to help provide books for an author visit. Or, as part of a reading incentive, take students on a field trip to the local ice-cream shop and then a visit to the local independent bookstore to purchase books for the school library.

The newspaper or school library website is a great way for the community to read about the school library program. Share information about programs, projects, or even some of the great resources available. One district of school librarians wrote a weekly book review column to share with the community. When the local newspaper stopped publishing the reviews, they moved the reviews to the district website for the community to continue to enjoy.

Consider having students post a podcast about the week in review at the school—highlighting, of course, some of the things happening in the school library. How about posting a video of the morning announcements out on the web each day? Use a blog to connect with a visiting author before he or she visits the school. The interaction might allow the community to participate in the discussion. Consider having the author do an evening presentation and inviting the community to join in.

Think in terms of how the school and community can work together. Are there projects or instructions that connect to the community where you can bring community members into the library as speakers? Are there project-based learning activities that classroom teachers and the school librarian are planning that lend themselves to encouraging the students to be a part of the community around them?

The community is another place to solicit volunteers. There may be retired people who are looking for a way to give back to the community, or maybe business professionals who have a free lunch once a week where they could donate their time. Think in terms of the jobs that need to be done and then see who might be the right volunteer to help. One librarian, at the beginning of the year, invited volunteers to sign up for the task they were most interested in helping with in the library.

School Librarians

School librarians sometimes feel isolated because there really is not any other person in the building who performs the same job. It becomes important to find other school librarians in the district, in the state, or even in other parts of the country where the school librarians can share situations/problems, brainstorm solutions, get new ideas, and build a network of friends.

When there are multiple school librarians in a school district, it is great to get together once in a while to talk and share. The concept is much like creating a professional learning community (PLC) of school librarian. According to www.allthingsplc.info/about/aboutPLC.php, a PLC is a group of educators working together to improve student achievement. They are focused on student learning, working collaboratively together, research best practices and implement them, and base all their decisions on results. District-wide coordinators will often take on the role to make sure that happens; but in districts without a coordinator, consider starting a group in the district. Perhaps start out with a professional book to get the conversation started. (There are many ideas and suggestions at the end of each chapter of the book.) Set protocols before starting, so that the gatherings are productive. For example,

✦ Conversations will stay positive.

✦ There is no whining.

✦ Work toward solutions.

✦ Share and take equally.

When there is only one school librarian in a district, it is important to branch out. Make contacts with other school librarians in the area. Perhaps a periodical gathering at a local restaurant would be a good way to begin sharing. If getting together face to face isn't possible, look into other ways to collaborate. Schedule a Google Hangout or Skype chat. Consider setting up a Facebook group where you can all share. Even simple e-mail messages back and forth can be helpful when you need someone to bounce an idea off.

One of the best ways to meet other school librarians is to attend the state school library association conferences. It is a great way to build a network of school librarian from all over the state with whom you can network for advice and ideas. National conferences allow the network to expand beyond the state boundaries.

Today's 21st-century technologies allow us to communicate and share in more ways than ever imaginable. People are just an e-mail away from all over the world. LM_Net has been connecting school librarians online since its inception in 1992. The e-mails bring questions and answers to the school librarian's inbox in droves each day or in a daily digest mode. Just searching the archives can provide a wealth of information for the school librarian. See http://www.lm-net.info/ for more information on subscribing and the archives.

Personal Learning Networks (PLN) with the onslaught of social media technologies are a great way to gain support and share ideas. Whether it be Twitter, Facebook, blogs, LinkedIn, webinars, or face-to-face interaction, all of those elements combine to form a PLN that the school librarian can rely on when he or she needs them. Look for more information about PLNs in Chapter 12.

Just as no two-school library programs are identical, no school librarian is exactly like another. As colleagues interact both face-to-face and virtual, take the best and incorporate it into the school library program. Everyone can take time to learn from each other and in the end students are the ones who benefit.

District Administrators

Depending on the size of the district the school librarian is working in, there may be a variety of district-level administrators that they will need and want to interact with in building the school library program. Some districts have school library program supervisors or coordinators. These people have dedicated jobs where they are working to be the school librarian's voice at the district level. The district school library coordinator paints the picture with district administrators about the role school librarians are playing. They can also be critical in removing barriers to the school librarian focusing on collaboration and instruction. A district library supervisor can also be leading with professional development, library administration, and other tasks that can help the building librarian focus on collaborating and working with students and teachers.

But, not all districts have that kind of support. Sometimes there is someone at the district level who has a small part of their job coordinating libraries, sometimes one of the librarians in the district take on a department chair role, and sometimes there is no one who is responsible for coordinating the libraries. There are all sorts of different scenarios. However, the key element is when there is not a direct, focused voice for school librarians, the building-level librarian has to work to make those connections. It could be conversations with those folks coordinating curriculum and instruction. It could be working with those that coordinate the other disciplines (language arts, math, etc.). It could be working with the finance and budget administrators that help to develop the district budget. It could be conversations with the superintendent about the vital role that school libraries play to the success of the district.

Each school librarian needs to take stock of what the proper channels and procedures are in their district. They need to know what the open avenues are for communication, and take advantage of those opportunities. It is important not to go around or not keep building- level administrators informed, but just as school librarians need to be leaders in their schools, they need to be some of the teacher leaders in their districts as well.

Instructional Coaches

Over the last several years, we've seen more and more districts hire instructional coach, reading specialists, technology integrators, and many other job titles with similar responsibilities. School librarians have often felt that some of these positions encroach on our roles and responsibilities. There may be some merit to that conversation. School librarians have to make sure they are demonstrating what they can do and putting that into action into their schools.

At the same time, some of this is beyond the control of the school librarian. So, instead of fighting, how can school librarians take advantage of these positions? Looks at people in these positions as key people to connect with for collaboration. By working with them on the professional development they are creating, working with them as they work with teachers, and being part of the conversations about how they are going to help move the school forward, the school librarian can be a vital component of the school's success.

Support Staff

Full- or part-time assistants are a major blessing in an elementary school. Having the support of assistants to assume clerical and technical roles makes it much easier for the school librarian to focus on the critical instructional role, working with students and teachers. Unfortunately, not every library is fortunate enough to have an assistant. The primary role of the school librarian should be instruction and working with students and teachers. This becomes difficult when there is no assistant to help. The school librarian will need to prioritize the various tasks and focus on the most important realization that some things just won't get done. If the books do not get back to the shelves quickly, life will go on. Maybe if people notice some things not being done, they may look for ways to help. The instructional role of the school librarian is always the most critical.

Working with assistants can sometimes be interesting—especially if the assistant had experience working in the library. The best plan is to try and bring them into the planning process. Be open and let them know what is going on, why it is happening, how they can help, and how the school librarian is going to support them. As they feel ownership in helping create and grow the program, they will work even harder to help reach the goal. Ask for their ideas and suggestions, too.

It is also a wise idea to be upfront and honest. For example, if the school librarian knows he or she has a control issue, share that with the assistant. If the assistant has a tendency to get overwhelmed quickly, he or she should tell the school librarian. The school librarian and the assistant have to work very closely together, so it is better to communicate early on to avoid problems later.

Consider scheduling a daily check in or weekly meeting with the assistant to preview the classes and projects coming up, the clerical tasks that will need to be done, and any other major events that might impact the school library. One librarian used a dry erase board so everyone had a clear idea of what projects needed to be done and how quickly they needed to be accomplished. Another school librarian used GoogleDocs and created a document that both the assistant and the librarian could use to plan projects and "to-do" lists. When both sides are knowledgeable about what is going on, it creates an environment where things can get done effectively and efficiently.

Volunteers

Volunteers cannot replace having paid staff, but they can help relieve some of the pressures from the school librarian. Volunteers can shelve books, check books out, repair books, cover and process books, put up bulletin boards, organize the book fair, and a host of other clerical type tasks freeing up the school librarian to work with students and instruction.

Not every volunteer can do every task. Quickly the school librarian will discover the best match between the volunteer and the tasks. Training takes some time up front, but a good volunteer can be worth it as the year progresses. Consider asking some of the volunteers from the previous year to help train the new volunteers. Also, consider not showing them everything at once, as that might be a daunting experience. Pick one task, train them, and then let them work on it. The trainings can build over time as the volunteer comes back. Some sources of volunteers include:

+ At back-to-school nights in the fall, request a few minutes to ask for volunteers. Focus on kindergarten parents because it may be possible to find a volunteer who will stay with the library during his or her child's entire time at the school.

+ Visit the PTA/PTO meeting and ask for assistance. Perhaps a parent would even take the lead in organizing the volunteer schedule.

+ Check with senior citizen centers or groups where seniors are looking for ways to stay active and involved.

Remember to check the district policy for volunteers. Some may require a background check before allowing adults to be in contact with students. It is important to be aware of any such rules or procedures first and sharing them with volunteers before the school librarian asks them to come and help.

Student Assistants

Student assistants can sometimes fill part of the void when there is a lack of volunteers or paid assistants. Students are often eager to help, and the school library provides a variety of things students can do to help. For example,

+ Set-up/shut down the library: turn on/off lights, shut down computers, and so on.
+ Dust shelves.
+ Trim lamination.
+ Die cut letters.
+ Run copies.
+ Load paper in printers.
+ Clean computer screens.
+ Pull books for teachers.

- ✦ Check-in/check-out books.
- ✦ Straighten shelves.
- ✦ Shelve books and other materials.

This is not an all-inclusive list, but an idea for a place to start. A lot depends on the students who volunteer and the level at which they can handle the tasks. Students can come in and volunteer 15–20 minutes at a time during one recess a week. This has little impact on the classroom and requires them to give up only one recess a week but still provides a chance for students to help. If each group has 5 to 6 students, that means over 30 students each week who could volunteer in the school library. Training time will be critical at the beginning of the year, but students can quickly become self-sufficient.

One example is a colleague, Kym Kramer, who set up her student volunteers (junior librarians) to go through a training system at the beginning of each year. She provided instruction on what she needed help with, guidance and practice, and there was an assessment before students found out what job they would be doing. She made sure, for several weeks during recess, that she was available for training and support; but once they got going, her junior librarians were able to run the clerical side of checking in, sorting books, and shelving. This left the librarian to focus the rest of the year on the instructional role and the library assistant to focus on more difficult clerical tasks. The vibe and atmosphere created was that this was part of giving back to the whole school community. It eventually led to a bigger school-wide initiative called Job Corp where most older students had some sort of job they were responsible for to keep the school running (Kramer 2016).

The school librarian will know what works best with his or her students and the school schedule in order to see what kind of help students might be to the school library.

School Library Advisory Committee

The sphere of influence references earlier in the chapter (Figure 2.1) shows how school librarians have to work and interact with all types of people. In order to make that influence effective, school librarians have to consider all those pieces and parts into making decisions about how the school library program grows and evolves. The school librarian will always be the one with the most experience about school library programs, but there is a wealth of knowledge in those other spheres that can greatly influence and improve a school library program. Involving those other spheres in the discussions about the vision can help create an even more successful school library program. Creating a school library advisory board is a great way to get influenced from all those spheres of people—the school librarian, principal, teachers, parents, students, and maybe some input from the community (a public library connections perhaps) who meet from time to time to develop a long-term plan, discuss policies and procedures, and work to solve any issues related to the school library program.

This group acts as an advisor to the school librarian and principal. It allows the various groups to have some input into decisions that are made. The library advisory committee is not the final decision maker, but rather it provides a forum for various stakeholders to share their feelings, thoughts, and ideas. This builds ownership for those people in the school library program because they are helping to shape it. For example, the group might discuss the viability of increasing the number of items children can check out. They might look at the school improvement plan and determine ways the school library program supports the plan.

The school library program belongs to the whole school; therefore, to include all those stakeholders in the various spheres will go a long way to building that culture and mind-set.

Setting Up an Advisory Committee

It may be difficult to get the entire group together especially if trying to coordinate with the schedule of parents. Consider meeting right before school so parents could participate before they go to work, or maybe meet right before a PTO meeting when parents are already planning to be in the building. Technology also provides ways to participate, so it might be that one uses Google Hangout or other similar products so parents could call into the meeting, or perhaps the meeting might work as using an e-mail discussion for input. Depending on the topic, a quick e-mail could be sent out and input quickly collected so a decision could be made.

In most elementary schools, the easiest way to set up the committee is to ask for a representative from each grade level, related arts teachers, and a special education teacher. One school opted to merge its technology committee and make it one group (Library/Technology Advisory Committee). This one committee could then talk about both topics since they are interrelated.

Advisory committees may also include parents and/or students depending on the grade configuration of the school and what kind of issues the committee is discussing. Bringing in the perspective from students and parents is always good because sometimes person from the outside looking in can see things that those inside looking out are missing.

In elementary schools, students may not be quite ready to be an active participant on a committee of adults. However, there are still ways to solicit their ideas and needs. Form a small student advisory committee and invite them to eat lunch in the school library once a month. Each month might have a different focus topic. Share it with the students ahead of time so they can be thinking of ideas. Perhaps one month the focus is on what kind of new books should the school librarian be searching for to add to the collection. Or, another month the conversation might center on activities to promote National School Library Month in April.

Another group that could be worth considering is creating a Friends of the Library group. Very similar to the role that a PTA/PTO takes on for the entire school, the Friends group could be a driving force to raise funds, solicit volunteers, and overall be a strong advocate for the school library. Check out the United for Libraries, a division of ALA, http://www.ala.org/united/friends for more information on how to start up a Friends group.

To conclude, with whatever kinds of committees or groups are formed, make sure that committee has a wide variety of personalities. It would be pointless to have a committee where everyone had the same opinion. Put some of those people on the committee who aren't strong library users. This just may be the opportunity needed to get them on board.

The school librarian's job requires one working with people of all types. One of the many number of things a school librarian can do to be successful is to build bridges to all colleagues. Show them the power and potential of what can happen by working with the school librarian! Amazing things will happen!

The job of the school librarian is very unique in a school because there are few positions where someone has to work with every person in the building. Working with such a range of people and personalities can be both exciting and stressful. The important thing is to know what each group needs and to work to see how the school library program can help them reach those needs.

Works Cited

All Things PLC: Research, Education Tools and Blog for Building a Professional Learning Community. Accessed May 9, 2009. http://www.allthingsplc.info/about/aboutPLC.php.

Hartzell, Gary. *Building Influence for the School Librarian: Tenets, Targets, and Tactics*, 2nd edition. Columbus, OH: Linworth Publishing, 2003.

Kramer, Kym. "Jr. Librarians." 2016. Via e-mail.

"United for Libraries." *United for Libraries Resources for Friends Groups*. Accessed 2016. http://www.ala.org/united/friends.

Further Reading

Bell, Mary Ann, Holly Weimar, and James L. van Roekel. *School Librarians and the Technology Department: A Practical Guide to Successful Collaboration*. Columbus, OH: Linworth Publishing, 2013.

Harlan, Mary Ann. *Personal Learning Networks: Professional Development for the Isolated School Librarian*. Columbus, OH: Libraries Unlimited, 2009.

Harvey, Carl. "Collaborating with the Coach." *School Library Connection* 1, no. 6 (2016): 9–10.

Harvey, Carl. *Educational Leadership: Coaching: The New Leadership Skill: The Coach in the Library*. Accessed July 31, 2016. http://www.Ascd.Org/publications/educational-leadership/oct11/vol69/num02/The-Coach-in-the-Library.Aspx.

Levitov, Deborah D., ed. *Activism and the School Librarian: Tools for Advocacy and Survival*. Columbus, OH: Libraries Unlimited, 2012.

McGhee, Marla W., and Barbara A. Jansen. *The Principal's Guide to a Powerful Library Media Program: A School Library for the 21st Century*. Columbus, OH: Linworth Publishing, 2010.

Techman, Melissa. "Beyond Junior Shelvers: Involving Creative Library Work." *School Library Connection* 1, no. 6 (February 2016): 43–44.

CHAPTER 3

Communication

One of the most important reasons that we communicate is to affect the behavior of other people.

— David F. Warlick, *Redefining Literacy 2.0*

Communication is at the heart of any successful school library program. The school librarian has to be able to clearly articulate the vision of the school library program to a variety of stakeholders, which often requires translation from "libraryese" into something the stakeholders can understand. It might also mean making multiple translations because each group has their own priorities, so it is important to show the school library program as it most impacts them.

Sometimes it is easy to assume that people see what the school library program is doing for kids and why it is important. The reality is that sometimes they have no idea. Therefore, it is essential to provide them with plenty of information in multiple formats. Talking face to face with someone is often an easy way to get one's message to him or her, but looking at communication through the 21st-century window, how can these new tools be used to talk with stakeholders? Gary Hartzell notes that people remember their school library program from when they were in school (Hartzell 2003, p. 94). This can be both good and bad. If that was not a positive experience (or was a long time ago), the school librarian will have to help paint them an image of what a 21st-century school library program looks like. The school librarian needs to leave no doubt that school library programs are a vital part of the school learning culture.

The previous chapter was organized around the people the school library program impacts. This chapter is organized by what vehicle the school librarian might use to delivery messages to the various stakeholders. Choosing the vehicle is based solely on how the audience best receives the information. It may vary from group to group and the school librarian will likely need to use a variety of communication strategies to get the message out.

Vehicles of Communication
Face to Face

One of the best ways to communicate is face to face. While e-mails or text messages might be faster, they lack the emotion and tone of the person's voice or the body language. Not to mention, some topics may be sensitive enough that having the information in print may not be appropriate.

Each administrator has a different style in how he or she operates. Some administrators have what is commonly called the open door policy. If the school librarian walks past the principal's office door and it is open, he or she knows he or she is free to interrupt to ask questions or have a conversation. If the door is closed, then the school librarian will need to find another time to talk. Typically, open door policies mean there is greater access to the administrator. Often time in one day the administrator may have multiple conversations with the school librarian on a wealth of topics.

The same can be said for conversations when the administrator comes in the school library. If the school librarian is not currently teaching a class, it may prove a good time for a conversation with the administrator. Many administrators make daily walks through the building and go into each space where children are learning. If it is hard to catch them with their open door policy, catching the administrator on the instructional walk through might be another opportunity.

Last, some administrators like schedules, appointments, and routine. They may not like to be interrupted. Depending on the administrator and school librarian, it may be wise to schedule a weekly or biweekly meeting to align calendars, discuss issues, and look ahead to future events.

Another group with which face-to-face meetings work well is teachers. While planning for instruction can happen over e-mail, a face-to-face conversation often works better to make sure the lesson has been completely thought out—especially for a project being done the first time. Some grade levels will meet together each week to plan out their next week's lessons. This is a perfect time for the school librarian to join in. He or she can offer suggestions and ideas for the teachers to think about as they are planning. One school librarian was talking with one of the technology assistants about how she never got a response for an e-mail. The school librarian knew her staff well enough to know that teacher functioned better with face-to-face conversations instead of e-mail. Knowing how people best receive information is critical.

Collaborative conversations sometimes work best face to face, too. In one school library, the school librarian had a library cookie jar. When the librarian's Grandmother moved out of her house, she thought the librarian should have this cookie jar that was purchased for her one year for Christmas. It was not really the librarian's style, but who is going to argue with their Grandma? So, the school librarian took it to school and put it in the workroom. Whenever the school librarian needed to interact with teachers (or knew the stress level was high in the

V.P. BARNES
ELEMENTARY SCHOOL LIBRARY

The mission of the Barnes Elementary Library is to prepare students for life-long learning, informed decision-making, a love of reading, and the use of information technologies.

The library operates on an open access schedule. Students may come to the library at any time -- individually, in small groups, or with their entire class -- to check out and return materials, to read for pleasure or information, to hear stories, or research topics for reports, using a variety of resources.

Collaborative Instruction

Instruction comes from the school librarian and the classroom teacher co-planning to create lessons that incorporate the *Standards for the 21st Century Learner* with the Academic Standards, in order to create authentic learning. By working together, the school librarian and the classroom teachers are able to both work with students as they use information and technology. Our lessons and projects help prepare students for the 21st Century by helping them become effective users of information and technology.

Online Databases

You can access online resources such as our computer catalog, student weblinks (great for homework help), and library information at: http://www.vpbarneselementary.k12.state.us/ Please notice the textbox along the right side for password for at home access to our online resources.

Special Programming

✦ The library program provides an annual visit from a children's author with funding provided by PTO. In addition, the library host two book fairs, and a variety of other special events and programming throughout the year.

✦ The State Library Association sponsors the State Book Award Program, and Barnes Elementary are active participants. Students who read or are read 12 of the 20 picture book titles, and students who read or are read 5 of the 20 intermediate titles by May 1st are eligible to vote for the title they liked best.

✦ Join the Barnes Library Birthday Book Club and celebrate a child's birthday (or the birthday of someone special to them). Bring in $5 to the library and he or she can choose a book to donate to our school from those selected by the school librarian. The child's name will be written in the book as a way to thank him or her.

Database Passwords
World Book Online
Login:
Password:
PebbleGo
Login:
Password:
TeachingBooks.net
Login:
Password:
BookFlix
Login:
Password:

Library Procedures

Number of Items: Students are limited to the number of items for which they can be responsible!

Check-Out Time Limit: Students may keep items for one week (chapter books for two weeks). Students are encouraged to return the items to the library as soon as they are finished so they can check out new ones!

Overdue Fines: There are no fines; however, students must return overdue items before new items may be checked out.

Lost Books: Students who lose or damage items beyond repair will be charged the replacement cost of the book. Parents may give permission for their children to check out more items while lost books are being sought by contacting Mr. Booker. Students who habitually lose books and do not pay for them will be limited to using items only at school.

Making Good Choices: The library strives to teach our students to be independent reading consumers. If you notice your child is bringing home materials at an inappropriate high or low level of difficulty, please discuss this with your child.

Volunteers

The library is always looking for adult volunteers to help shelve books, prepare new materials, and other tasks. If you are interested in helping, please contact one of our Media-Technology Assistants at 111.1111 ext. 111.

Questions or Comments?

Please contact Mr. Booker, School Librarian at 111.1111, ext. 110 or mr.booker@vpbarneselementary.k12.state.us

Figure 3.1 Sample Library Brochure.

building), the librarian would fill the cookie jar and send out an e-mail. The teachers would come running. The conversations around the cookie jar led to some great collaborations and was amazing for building relationships with the staff.

At the beginning of each school year, most buildings host a back-to-school night. The schedule and format vary, but the point is to get parents into the school to give them a preview of the year ahead. At one such school, each grade level did an hour presentation. It took three nights to get them all completed, but the school librarian attended and spoke at each one of those meetings. She explained circulation policies to the parents, talked about some of the collaborative projects that their children will be experiencing in the coming years, shared passwords for access to library databases from home, and puts out a call for volunteers to help in the school library. This face-to-face meeting is a positive and perfect opportunity to connect with parents. See Figure 3.1 for a sample library flyer for parent night. If the school doesn't have such an event, look for other opportunities. Maybe on Meet-the-Teacher night, set-up a booth in the lobby or near the library to promote the library. Make sure the library is open during an open house and have ways to draw people into the library for conversation. Perhaps send home the flyer as part of (or separately) from the school newsletter to highlight the procedures in the library.

Besides back-to-school night, most schools also have a PTA or PTO that helps support the school. These organizations of dedicated parents and teachers are the groups that organize, run, and fund countless programs in the school. They support the school with volunteers, enrichment programming, and are the "go-to" people when the school needs additional support or help. These groups are also a potential funding source for the school library, so at one school the school librarian attends the meetings each month. From time to time, she shares some of the programs going on in the library and thanks the PTA/PTO for supporting them.

Print

In the 21st century, the advent of technology and the green movement has caused us to rethink the use of paper. The amount of trees saved in addition to the amount of money saved have made school librarians (and more important school district administrators) rethink things like a traditional newsletter to faculty, a newsletter home to students, or a monthly/annual report to administrators. This is not to say all those items have gone away, but rather the school librarian has been looking at alternative ways to share that same information. By looking for alternative ways, school librarians can showcase technology skills while at the same time model "being green" and doing their part to help save the environment.

One school librarian makes a packet every year for the teachers giving them all the information they need about the school library—forms, procedures, passwords, and so forth. The packet's format seems to change every year. There were folders, binder packets, and bags. The variety was to make it different each year even if some of the information was the same to show teachers that this was a new start. It started out in print but had been moving toward digital. The newer version could be Google Drive folder where teachers will be able to quickly access the information all year long, and the librarian can easily update it as things change. See Figure 3.2 for a listing of what was in the back-to-school packet.

Back-to-School Packet for Teachers and Staff

Here are some possible examples of resources to give teachers and staff at the beginning of the year. This gives them a quick reference guide to library and technology resources.

Quick Reference Guide for Teachers and Staff
Table of Contents

Information
- Library Procedures and Fact Sheet
- Important Dates
- Library & Technology Questions—Who Do I Ask?
- What Can a Teacher Expect of a School Librarian?
- Collaboration Connections
- Library Integration Guide or Curriculum
- Textbook Procedures

Instructional Resources
- Technology Resources (Software and Hardware)
- Guide to Online Resources
  - Library Webpage
  - Library Computer Catalog
  - State-Wide Databases
  - World Book Online
  - Database purchased by the District or Building
  - eBook resources
  - Schools Blogs
- State Book Award Nominees
- Quick Online Reference Guide to Stick to Computer

Figure 3.2 Back-to-School Packet.

E-Mails

Educators are bombarded today with e-mails of all kind from all types of people—administrators, parents, students, and yes, even the school librarian. It has become a vital link to everyone in the school. While some educators are more conscientious about reading their e-mail than others, the same could be said for the print newsletters that used to be copied onto paper. E-mail is not any less effective but rather just another way to send out the information.

E-mail can be used as a tool to deliver important information like schedules, overdue notices, and so on. It can also be a tool to provide professional development as well as a way to highlight new resources available in the school library. See Figure 3.3 for e-mail examples. Schedules for enrichment programs, notices about technology problems, or just an FYI that overdue notices are going home are some of the countless uses for staff e-mail. It is a quick and easy way to send to everyone the details they need to be aware of for a variety of topics.

Many automation systems now have an option to e-mail out overdue notices. Sending them directly to the patrons' e-mail box allows them to see what they still have checked out and avoids printing it out on paper. There are a lot of privacy issues that arise because, in most cases, at the elementary level, the e-mail address the school has belongs to a parent or guardian. School librarians (and librarians of all type) have always been advocates for protecting students' right to privacy. However, under the Family Educational Rights and Privacy Act (FERPA), school library circulation records meet the legal definition of "education records," so if a parent were to ask, they can have access to them.

Should teachers have access to what students check out? FERPA states that those school officials with a "legitimate educational interest" may have access. Would a teacher's current class fit under those guidelines? As more of these tools and features make it easier to share information, school librarians always have to be clear about what they are sharing, the reason why the individual wants the information, and whether they should be sharing it. Just as most automation systems have the option to turn off tracking the patron's history, which therefore helps protect their privacy, school librarians need to think carefully about e-mailing overdues because this action impacts a student's privacy as well.

Professional development is another option for e-mail. Those monthly newsletters the school librarian used to run off on the copier are now sent via e-mail instead of printed out. Sent as a PDF file or pasted right into the e-mail itself, the newsletters contain important updates for the faculty, directions for using new pieces of technology, and links to websites and books that support school improvement goals. Website such as Smores.com is another option for designing newsletters electronically. Newsletters might also contain things like a calendar of author birthdays, important information about new technology, and a list of collaborative projects. They continue to need to be short and succinct for staff to read them, but e-mail allows them to be sent without the wasted paper. See Figure 3.4 for a newsletter example.

Other things that can be sent via e-mail include a weekly website or random resource. Connect it back to the school improvement plan and academic standards. It could be an online tool,

> To: Principal
> From: School Librarian
> CC: Classroom Teacher
> Re: Awesome Project
>
> Just wanted to share what a great project we did with Mr. Jones classes this week. His students came up with something about the Civil War they wanted to know more about. Each day their class came to the library to work on their projects. Students really had to think about what terms to use while searching for information on their individual projects. I can't wait to see their final projects when they share them in a couple of weeks. You are welcome to join us in the library to listen to their final presentations.
>
> Thanks,
>
> School Librarian

Tips for E-Mailing your Administrator

- ✦ Keep them short and on one topic.
- ✦ Phrase all requests in a manner of "How will this benefit kids?"
- ✦ Invite the administrator to the library often.
- ✦ Make sure that all your e-mails are not negative; share good news, too!
- ✦ Make sure to cc: teachers on e-mails you send the administrator praising them.
- ✦ Carbon copy the principal on e-mails when you send new resources, new books, tips, and ideas.
- ✦ For sensitive topics or when the potential to be misunderstood is apparent, send an e-mail requesting to speak in person.
- ✦ If you are writing an e-mail in response to a problem or concern and you are upset or angry, make sure *not* to send it right away. Take time to cool down and rewrite. It may even be better to calm down and make an appointment to discuss rather than put something in writing.

> To: All Staff
> From: School Librarian
> Re: Random Resource
> This week I just finished The Best Book Ever by Writing Author. It was amazing. I saw so many connections to our standards, and it would be a wonderful read-aloud for 3rd or 4th grade. The language and storytelling are just amazing.
> The book centers around the beach, so I found this great website of resources to support using this novel. I put together a Symbaloo of curated resources to support using this book in the classroom.
> Happy Reading and Surfing!
> Academic Standards: English/LA
> School Improvement Plan: Literacy

Ideas for e-mails to send teachers:

- ✦ Weekly website
- ✦ Highlight a new book and way to use
- ✦ Directed e-mails to grade levels or Departments with New Resources
- ✦ Directed e-mails to grade levels or Departments with Ideas for Collaborative Projects
- ✦ Monthly newsletter

Figure 3.3 Sample E-Mails.

The Not-So-Quiet Library

(Following are some possible article ideas. You could also use these as heading for blog postings. Try and keep your newsletter to one page front/back. Rotate columns depending on what is happening in your library and the story you need to tell!)

Collaboration Corner—Share the great projects happening in your library—a great place to recognize teachers who are working with you.

Coming Soon—Here you can promote upcoming events such as the book fair or an author visit.

I Found It on the Web—Share a website such as an online collaborative tool and how you might use it with students.

A Picture Is Worth a Thousand Words—Highlight a new picture book and how you might use it in the classroom.

It's a Novel Idea—Highlight a new novel and how you might use it in the classroom.

Calendar—Share library events, upcoming projects, and/or author birthdays!

Quotable Quote—Find great quotes from children's literature or quote books to share!

What's New in the Library?—Print a list of new resources in the library. Time this with a new book days where teachers can come down and see the books on the list.

Just the Facts—Share with them some stats about the library. How many books have been checked out? How many classes have used the library?

Clip It; Save It!—Share a short professional development tip such as how to use a database or the library computer catalog.

Figure 3.4   Sample Newsletter.

School Library ~ Principal Update **Date: _____**	
Collaboration ◆ Kindergarten— ◆ 1st Grade— ◆ 2nd Grade— ◆ 3rd Grade— ◆ 4th Grade— ◆ Related Arts, Special Education—	In this box, include all the collaborative lessons and projects. This is a great place to mention teachers who are working with the school librarian.
General Media/Tech Information ◆ ◆ ◆ ◆	In this box, include administrative tasks and work and projects. Make sure to include the work your support staff is doing as well.
Professional Activities ◆ ◆ ◆ ◆ ◆	In this box, highlight conferences and workshops attended, visitors to your library, articles published, and so on.
Upcoming Activities ◆ ◆ ◆ ◆ ◆	In this box, give a preview of the month ahead. This could include projects, special events, workshop you are attending or presenting.

Library Media Center Statistics

Faculty: _____
(____ / 50 staff members)
Students: _____
(____ / 460 students)
Classes in for Instruction:

_____

Broken Down by Month—Student Circulation

August	
September	
October	
November	
December	
January	
February	
March	
April	
May	

In this box, include some statistics. These will vary depending on the level and your administrator. Use those statistics that speak about your school improvement goals.

Figure 3.5 Monthly Report.

a new book and strategies for using it, or maybe just a reminder of something already in the library.

Reports to administrator are now on e-mail as well. A monthly report to an administrator might include: classes that have collaborated with the school librarian, a list of administrative tasks completed by the school librarian and support staff, a calendar of events that happened during the previous month, and a list of upcoming events. Circulation stats are also a good addition to this short report. The annual report also could be sent via e-mail or uploaded onto the web for all to see. See Figure 3.5 for an example of a monthly report and Figure 3.6 for an example of an annual report. Share these reports with the staff as well. They can be useful to show what a school library program is all about to many different stakeholders.

School district, teachers, and librarians have also been using options such as School Messenger, Class Messenger, and Remind 101 to name a few where they can send e-mail or text blasts out to parents. This is a great way to promote events in the library as well or solicit volunteers for the book fair. Make sure to follow the district's policies before using.

People are bombarded with them everyday, so keep the message short and focused so they quickly can get the information they need and be willing to read it. Be sure to not go overboard in the number of messages too. Keep them short, succinct, and to the point.

School Library Webpage

The school library webpage is not only an amazing communication opportunity but also one that has seen drastic change in the last several years with additional technologies that schools are using. Initially, a one-way format where the school librarian could share with students, parents, teachers, and administrators, school library websites became a place for interaction between the school librarian and their patrons. In schools with learning management systems (LMS), the librarian also needs to create a presence for students and staff to access library resources via the LMS. Typically the LMS is locked to users, so it is important the library have a presence both inside the LMS and outside on the web. So, the next few years may continue to see changes in how the school librarian makes his or her virtual presence known.

The classic school library website has a link to the school library catalog, links for student projects, links to databases, and a space to advertise library events. Just as the school library is the hub of the school, the website is the hub of the school's online presence.

As more interactive tools became available, school librarians have been able to use blogs, wikis, podcast, and embedded widgets to make their web presence more dynamic and interactive. It allows the user to interact with the school librarian and other users and as before gives the student access to the school library resources beyond the library walls. Digital curation tools such as Symbaloo, Pearl Trees, and many others allow school librarians to organize and expand the resources available from their website.

Briefly summarize one collaborative project you started this school year.

What connections has the library media program made to the building school improvement plan?

+ Literacy

+ Math

What role has the library media program played in professional development?

What were some of the major highlights from this school year?

What plans/goals are planned for the library program?

Our goals for next year include:

Just the Facts

How many total items circulated this year?	
To Students?	
To Staff?	
Leveled Libraries?	
How many classes used the library facility? (Total Number)	
How many collaborative projects, units, or lessons between the school librarian and classroom teacher?	

Consider ways to make the report more interesting. Make it a comic book, a video, use an online collaborative tool, etc. Variety can make it more interesting for the read. Include images. Take full advantage of our creativity.

Figure 3.6 Annual Report.

The website is also a great place to share what is happening in the school library. Embed a Google Slide in the website to scroll through images of what is happening, include a blog of all the activities going on, or embed a Twitter feed so stakeholders can see all the tweets of what is happening in the library. The possibilities are endless.

Many districts now use outside firms to design and provide tools for quick and easy edits of a website. Common design and layout, consistency of where information is, and a more appealing visual for the school district is often the rationale for using a web designer or vendor. This can be difficult when the school librarian who previously had a separate site or is just a little more creative than a template might allow now has to conform his or her site to match the district style. However, keep in mind the goal of the website and how you can make it work even with a district-style template.

If the district doesn't provide webspace or a site, check district policies about setting up websites, blogs, and wikis on space other than that owned by the district. Weebly, Wix, and Google sites are all great options; however, some schools have procedures and policies in place that will need to be followed or reviewed before creating a school library website.

Also the school librarian will want to make sure the school library website is easily accessible to students. A main link off the school page is the most appropriate but sometimes can be difficult to convince administrators. If that is the case, focus on access for students, faculty, and parents. Focus on how much online resources are available (especially paid databases) and how the one place for resources in the building is the school library, so the one place for all the resources online should be the link to the school library online.

One school librarian made sure the library website was the homepage of every Internet browser in the building so that students had easy access (It compiled with the district policy, as the policy was: the homepage had to be one of the pages of the district website but did not specify which one!). The district always marveled at how the library website of that school always topped with the most hits than any other pages in the district. Create posters that the school librarian can give to teachers to direct students to the school library website. Bookmarks or other resources can be nice guides for students. Include a QR code for easy access via mobile devices.

As mentioned earlier, learning management systems are becoming more and more popular in schools at all levels. This is a great opportunity for conversations with the technology staff about how the school library is connected. Begin those conversations from the start of implementation. How will students access the online resources available? How can students get access to the school librarian for help via the learning management system? Be bold in pursuing the ways that the school library program needs to be represented in the learning management system.

It is possible that with the learning management system, the focus of that access would be for students and staff. The focus of the website then becomes more geared toward parents and the community. Consider the audiences who will be accessing those resources. Consider how the two can work together (to make the school librarian's life easier) as the school librarian won't want to be spending hours updating two different spaces if it can be avoided.

Finally, no matter what kind of online presence you have, make sure to consider the use of it by all types of users. http://wave.webaim.org/ is an online tool you can use to check on the accessibility of the website. Drs. Annette Lamb and Larry Johnson on their eduscapes site have a whole page focused on accessibility—http://eduscapes.com/arch/13.htm. Consider, too, there are all sorts of disabilities—so colors, layout, and content are all important choices when designing a webpage.

These online tools provide a plethora of new options for sharing what is happening in the school library. Take advantage of them not only as a tool for students to express their learning but also as a vehicle to get the positive message out about the school library.

Video

School libraries that have a morning announcement show can use that to advertise what is happening in the school library. Promote an author coming to visit, or book talk some of the new titles in this year's book fair. Have students come on and share the projects they've been working on both in the classroom and the library.

Use the video format as an advocacy tool not only for what is happening in the library but you can also utilize it to be a way to share about other departments and areas in the school. Invite the principal to come and share important announcements. The nurse could provide health tips. The counselor could talk about character education tips. Maybe the P.E. teacher could focus on exercises each day. There are lots of options and ideas to consider when you have the video format.

Videos can be filmed and posted on the web for others to learn about what is happening at school, too. Make sure that any video posted to the web adheres to copyright guidelines. Putting information out on the web is a public performance, so any music should be royalty free and the students must have created any images or text. If there are any items that are copyrighted, they need to be edited out or permission from the copyright holder granted before posting them online. In addition, videos with students' images and work must comply with all the district guidelines for posting online.

Social Media

The use of social media continues to rise. Twitter, Facebook, and Instagram are all popular vehicles for communication. As adults tend to move into spaces, students move on to other tools. Most of the user guidelines for these tools also limit access or prohibit students in the elementary school age bracket. So, does this mean an elementary school librarian can ignore them? While the students aren't there (or shouldn't be on them because of their usage guidelines), parents, staff members, and the community are using these resources. They are also perfect avenues for building a personal learning network (PLN). Connecting with school librarians and other educators from across the country can be invaluable as the school librarian develops the program.

A Facebook page for the parents could be a great way to keep them informed about library events, new strategies for working with their students at home, resources available in print and online from the school library, and even sharing just the projects and work going on in the school library. The same would be true for a Twitter account. Most people pick the tool they like, so it is impossible to catch everyone with just one. Multiple options and tools have to be used to get the message out to everyone.

No matter how you decide to use the social media tools, make sure to check what the district policies are—especially when it comes to posting pictures online. However, it is important that school librarians take the lead in implementing and utilizing these tools to connect and communicate with parents and the community.

Online Tools

There are other online tools that might be useful for communication as well. How about a GoogleDoc of new resources in the library that is updated periodically? Consider Google-Forms as a great way to collect data for the school librarian. Students can use the form to request new materials, check in/out of the library, or teachers can use it to make recommendation for professional development sessions.

The Future

It is almost impossible to know what the next big thing in communication and technology options might be. School librarians have to be willing to expand and explore new ideas. They have to be willing to take time to learn these new tools and be ready to use them to spread the word about what is happening in the school library. Make sure to follow any school or district guidelines with these tools as well. It may be the school librarian will need to help take the lead in creating or revising existing policies.

School librarians need to take advantage of all the communication tools in their arsenals. These tools are the vehicle to get the message out about what the school library program does and how it impacts student achievement. Communication is critical for working with all the variety of stakeholders. As the 21st century brings new tools and communication formats, school librarians need to look for how these tools can be used to communicate!

Works Cited

Hartzell, Gary. *Building Influence for the School Librarian: Tenets, Targets, and Tactics*, 2nd edition. Columbus, OH: Linworth Publishing, 2003.

Warlick, David F. *Redefining Literacy 2.0*, 2nd edition. Columbus, OH: Linworth Publishing, 2009.

AASL Educators of School Librarians Section. *Preservice Toolkit for Principals and Teachers*. American Association of School Librarians, 2016. Accessed April 19, 2016. http://www.ala.org/aasl/sites/ala.org.aasl/files/content/aaslissues/toolkits/Preservice Educators_Toolkit_FINAL_2016-03-17.pdf.

Adams, Helen R. *Ensuring Intellectual Freedom and Access to Information in the School Library Media Program*. Santa Barbara, CA: Libraries Unlimited, 2008.

Adams, Helen R. *Protecting Intellectual Freedom and Privacy in Your School Library*. Santa Barbara, CA: Libraries Unlimited, 2013.

Baule, Steven M., and Julie E. Lewis. *Social Networking for Schools*. Santa Barbara, CA: Linworth Publishing, 2012.

Berger, Pam, and Sally Trexler. *Choosing Web 2.0 Tools for Learning and Teaching in a Digital World*. Santa Barbara, CA: Libraries Unlimited, 2010.

Church, Audrey P. *Your Library Goes Virtual*. Worthington, OH: Linworth Publishing, 2006.

Coombs, Karen A., and Jason Griffey. *Library Blogging*. Worthington, OH: Linworth Publishing, 2008.

Fontichiaro, Kristin. *Podcasting at School*. Santa Barbara, CA: Libraries Unlimited, 2008.

Hauser, Judy. *The Web and Parents: Are You Tech Savvy?* Santa Barbara, CA: Libraries Unlimited, 2009.

Lewis, Kathryn. "KQ Blog: Annual Reports—It's That Time of Year." *Knowledge Quest Blog*. April 18, 2016; Accessed April 19, 2016. http://knowledgequest.aasl.org/annual-reports-time-year/.

Magi, Trina, and Martin Garnar, eds. *Intellectual Freedom Manual*. Chicago, IL: ALA Editions, 2015.

Martin, Ann M., and American Association of School Librarians. *Empowering Leadership: Developing Behaviors for Success*. Chicago, IL: American Association of School Librarians, 2014.

Scales, Pat R. *Protecting Intellectual Freedom in Your School Library: Scenarios from the Front Lines*. Chicago, IL: American Library Association, 2009.

Teehan, Kay. *Wikis: The Educator's Power Tool*. Santa Barbara, CA: Linworth Publishing, 2010.

CHAPTER 4

Curriculum and Instruction

We must take every step necessary to put our school library at the center of the school universe—and the most essential step of all is collaboration.

— Toni Buzzeo, "Collaborating from the Center of the School Universe"
Library Media Connection

The instructional component of the school library program continues to grow and expand. The American Association of School Librarians (AASL) standards outline the mission of the school library program as helping students (and staff) be prepared for finding, using, evaluating, creating, and sharing information.

AASL's standards also provide guidance for what students need to know by the time they leave high school. The school librarian's job is to integrate those standards into the instruction and curriculum happening in schools. Through collaboration, the school librarian embeds the AASL standards within the content standards to create rich learning experiences for students.

Standards

Standards are a hot topic in education. In the first edition, the focus was on state standards. In the years since then, there was a move to the Common Core State Standards (CCSS) with the goal of providing a unified set of standards across the country in language arts and mathematics to a backlash to the Common Core Standards by states that had adopted them and subsequently rejected them and returned to a state standards model. In the beginning, all but just a few states joined the CCSS movement. Now several states have backed out of the standards and the assessment and have created their own sets of standards that seem to mirror the CCSS.

In the field of school librarianship, the AASL publishes two different sets of standards and guidelines—one focused on school library instruction (student standards) and one set of standards for school library programs (what does the library need to meet the student standards). The last set of standards was published in 2007, and AASL is in the middle of an update/revision that is scheduled to be published in the fall of 2017.

Beyond the AASL standards and the state standards, there are many other standards published by the International Society for Technology in Education, International Literacy Association, and the Next Generation Science Standards just to name a few. Some states adopt these national standards as their own, while others do not. Whether they are adopted in the state or not, it is important to be aware of the national conversations of these various organizations. Many of the resources they provide for their standards can be useful in curriculum development in the district.

So, there are a great variety of standards available. It is crucial that school librarians know their state and/or district standards. They also need to be well versed in the AASL standards. Curriculum, collaboration, instruction, and assessment are all developed with those standards in mind. School librarians have to be leaders in understanding what is expected, so they can help drive curriculum. As school librarians collaborate with teachers, librarians begin with the content standards teachers are expected to cover, and then working together the school librarian includes the AASL standards. Teaching the content in the AASL standards isn't an extra but rather embedded in what the classroom teacher already has to teach.

Sometimes when working with teachers, having a framework is helpful. Sample lessons and ideas of what the standards mean can help create ideas and spark conversation. For example, Illinois Standards Aligned Instruction for Libraries (ISAILs), http://www.islma.org/ISAIL.htm, was created by the Illinois School Library Media Association Standards Committee to demonstrate the cross-curricular value of school libraries. The AASL standards also have examples of what the standards look like at each level. It is unlikely that teachers and school librarians would implement these projects exactly as written, but they provide ideas for creating lessons and units while scaffolding the format. When building that collaborative relationship, sometimes having some models or examples to share of potential can shine a light on the potential that collaboration can provide.

Curriculum Development

As states update their content standards, as textbooks change, as new teachers are hired into a grade level, and as new resources become available, there are constant changes and alterations to the curriculum at a grade level. They may require subtle changes that are just altered as a grade-level plan each week, or they may need complete overhauls of the yearlong plan. The school librarian is an active part of that planning because there is great potential to influence the plan and to help teach the plan.

Some schools provide their teachers with a day or two each year or during the summer to work on updating their curriculum. Sometimes this happens without any time or financial support from the district. Teachers take on the curriculum design themselves during their free time. However the revisions are taking place, the school librarian needs to be included in those planning sessions. During those revisions, there is potential that the school librarian can provide additional or new resources teachers can use, he or she can suggest projects that bring in the AASL standards, or can help provide ways teachers can utilize technology as part of their plans.

These planning sessions work as a two-way communication street as the curriculum is developed and revised. There is more time to plan out projects and activities to support these standards. There is great opportunity to talk about what resources might be needed to meet the needs to the adjustments. When the school librarian has advanced warning to find resources and plan instruction, the more helpful the school librarian can be when teachers are ready to implement the revised curriculum.

Consider the school where the principal moved several teachers to different grade levels. One level in particular had all new teachers. The school librarian made it a priority to attend those planning sessions. The school librarian was on the ground floor of designing and implementing that curriculum that resulted in successful collaborative experiences.

At another school, the school librarian participated in a training session with the literacy coach. The grade level was working to completely revamp their units of study. This was a great opportunity for the school librarian to be in on the ground floor of curriculum development. Not only was the unit tied better to the grade-level standards but they were also able to embed and integrate the school library into their units.

Assessment

Just as the librarian's role is vital for planning and implementing instruction, the librarian's role in assessment is equally crucial. It seems logical that if the skills and information school librarians teach are important, they should also be assessed. This does not necessarily mean students need a library grade but rather as part of a project, there should be evaluation of the process and the work students did while working with the school librarian. Just as the planning and teaching should be collaborative, so should the assessment (Harada and Yoshina 2005, pp. 5–6).

Be upfront with students that they will be required to turn in materials that support their work during the project. Students could turn in a journal detailing notes of what they did each day. It could be a flowchart that shows their process—both success and failures. It could be all the rough drafts, note cards, and bibliographies. Whatever it is, the documentation should be sufficient to determine if the student was learning the skills needed. See Figure 4.1 for a sample assessment. Project components should be assessed, and the final project grade should reflect the process as well as final product. The school librarian and classroom teacher may want to do all the assessment together, or they may consider dividing up pieces and parts of the project so each take a role in grading. For example, the school librarian might assess the research piece (gathering and evaluating sources) while the classroom teacher assesses the final project.

Rubric: Frog Blogging

Original Post		10		5		0
		The student posted a complete response. It included details from their research. Their opinions were supported with data.		The student posted a reasonable response. It included some details from their research. Their opinions, however, were not supported with data.		The student did not post a complete response. There were no facts from their research.
Comments		10				0
		The student used data to respond to their classmates' posts. They responded to at least five of their classmates.		The student used data to respond to their classmates' posts. They responded to at least three of their classmates.		The student did not use data to respond to their classmates' posts. They responded to fewer than one people.
Responsibility		10				0
		All of the students' replies were appropriate. They were respectful when dissenting and treated their classmates with respect.		Most of the students' replies were appropriate. They were respectful with dissenting and treating their classmates with respect.		The student did not reply appropriately. They were disrespectful to their classmates.
Students' Total Score						

Figure 4.1   Sample Assessment.

Students need feedback throughout their project. Knowledge of results is motivating. The feedback should be timely and specific (Harada and Yoshina 2005, p. 5). To be successful, everyone needs to know how they are doing and assessing student work provides students with that feedback. In addition, educators need to know whether the methods are working. If students miss something, it is important to reteach the skill. If school librarians are not assessing what the students are learning, how does one know if students are understanding, if they need more support, or if the skill needs to be retaught to the entire class?

Assessment allows us to check if the skills are used in real-world applications in ways that promote transference of the skills. It is also an important piece of the puzzle because it provides data that helps to tell the story of the school library program. The story it tells is about the learning going on in the school library. It is important to collect this data not only to impact what the school librarian does with students but also to impact how others view the role of the school library program in the school.

Standardized Tests

Every school across the country has at least one form of a standardized test. For those with the CCSS that might be the Partnership for Assessment of Readiness for College and Careers (PARCC) or Smarter Balanced assessment depending in which state you reside. These multiple choice and written response tests are how schools are judged to be effective or not effective according to state and national legislation.

As schools develop their curriculum and instruction, teachers are narrowing in on the standards that will be covered on annual exams. They are focused on the areas their students did not succeed in and looking for ways to improve. These data points drive the school improvement process because the results have a huge impact on the school. These data points control the ways schools get money, staff, curriculum initiatives, and district or state mandates imposed on them.

No matter what one's opinion is about these exams, the school librarian needs to be part of the group that analyzes and looks at the test results. The school librarians should be part of the data team in their building. These data teams are not only looking at the test data but also making programmatic decisions that could impact the school library program. If the school librarian is at the table during these discussions, the school librarian can offer input and suggestions as the school determines how to move forward.

Being aware of the testing data is also an important collaboration tool. When working with teachers, the school librarians are able to suggest ways that through their collaborative projects they can integrate the skills the students need for the standardized test, too. As the pressures mount, teachers often begin to back away from projects because they believe them to be too labor intensive. The teacher will comment they don't have time because they have to prepare for the test. The school librarian's role is to help teachers see how they can still prepare for the test by using a project-based method instead.

For example, take a written response-type question where students have to read a nonfictional passage and then write a response. Those responses are looking for the student to pull evidence from the passage to support their writing. Because of the data analysis, the school librarian already knows that this is an area where students in his or her building need additional support. So, the school librarian uses this as an opportunity to help the fourth teacher design a project where students are going to use strategies for reading informational text. He or she used her knowledge of the data as an opening to work with the teacher on a necessary skill for students.

The students choose from a cart of new books any informational book related to topics they are studying. The students read it and write a book review. Students have to support their opinions of the book by pulling out information and examples from the text. They have to evaluate if the information in the book is accurate. Perhaps even cross checking the information in another source. The students upload their reviews into the library catalog or the library website to share with others allowing them to share their opinions and thoughts with an authentic audience.

The activity serves the purpose of practicing the skill for the test but at the same time does it in such a way as to keep the students engaged and connected to the classroom. The school librarian has taken the lead in helping to model using informational text strategies as well as helping prepare the students for their standardized test.

Collaborative Teaching

For school librarians, the way to combine the AASL standards and whatever curriculum/state standards used together is through collaboration. A few years ago an experienced teacher moved to a new school district. Each Monday, his grade level would sit down to plan out the next week. In addition to the fourth-grade teachers, the school librarian and special education teacher also attended the planning sessions. While he was used to collaborating with the other teachers at his grade level, he was amazed to see the connection with the school librarian and special education teachers. Not only were they there just to listen about the week ahead but they also contributed ideas and strategies. They scheduled research projects, considered ideas for ways to use technology, maximized their use of resources, and worked together as a team to benefit the learning experiences planned for the students. Finally after about a month, he looked at the others who had been joining the planning and said, "Do you guys come every week?" In his previous school there had been no interaction with the school librarian or resource teachers. This was a new environment and he so appreciated the team approach to their lesson planning and the influence the resource teachers and the school librarian have on their planning, so it was a pleasant surprise for him.

Collaboration, as defined by Toni Buzzeo in *The Collaboration Handbook*, is when "the partners have a prolonged and interdependent relationship. They share goals, have carefully defined roles in the process, and plan much more comprehensively. Units and projects are team-planned, team-taught, and team-assessed" (Buzzeo 2008, p. 30). There is so much power in what can be offered to students by combining the skills, knowledge, and expertise of the school librarian and the classroom teacher. Collaboration is a two-way street. When just starting out, it often seems like the school librarian is the one driving and pushing to work with teachers. However, once the model is in place and there is an understanding of the potential, teachers come to the school librarian to initiate and plan projects. When you combine the power of two educators together, the impact for student learning increases. Students have two educators planning with their best ideas, and the instruction is better because instead of one teacher, students are getting two teachers. One of the obstacles to collaboration often mentioned is the school library schedule. The debate about flexible versus fixed scheduling has long raged in the field. Chapter 7 of this book discusses more about the battle of reality versus ideal, but no matter what type of schedule exists in the school library, collaboration is critical for student learning. The model of teaching library skills in isolation is not effective.

No matter what schedule the school library program operates on, teachers and school librarians should be working together. (The same applies to related arts teachers [art, music, P.E.]!). It can be very powerful for students when everyone plans together allowing for the bridging of skills and knowledge. Powerful connections can be made. For example, consider the following primary-level scenario. All of these teachers sat down together to plan a unit focused around the pond biome. The overarching science standards were the link. Students were to know and understand what a biome was, who lived in the biome, and how they worked together for survival. Each teacher was able to take his or her own standards to adapt and design content around a centralized theme. These connections provided a learning experience for students where everything related to each other. Following is a quick summary of what it looked like in the various rooms.

✦ **In the classroom:** Students completed a K-W-L chart about frogs and pond life. They take this with them to their other related arts classes to see if they can make connections to art, music, physical education, etc.

✦ **In art:** Students created images of frogs talking about color and perspective.

✦ **In music:** Students used instruments to recreate sounds heard around a pond. They accessed a database such as PebbleGo to find what their animals sound like.

✦ **In physical education:** Students try to mimic how animals around the pond move (jumping, hopping, crawling, and flying). Students worked in teams to create an exercise to teach the whole school based on a pond animal.

✦ **In the school library:** Students researched about frogs and determined what they had to have in their environment to survive. Students then choose another animal to research and had to determine whether their animal could survive in the pond environment or not. They shared their findings on the class wiki. (In a flexible environment, the classroom teacher and school librarian would do this together. In a fixed environment, the librarian would teach this on his or her own, which might take a little longer.)

✦ **In the computer lab:** Students developed a blog where they can post what they've learned and began to think about ways to protect the frog's habitat or environment.

✦ **Back in the classroom:** Students talked about fact or fiction reading text of both types based on frogs. Students also reflected on what they've learned and determine if there is still more information they need.

✦ **Assessment:** The classroom teacher, school librarian, and related art teachers all assessed students' progress during this unit. Each project has a rubric developed by the teacher but shared with others. So, for example, in the computer lab there was a rubric like the one in Figure 4.1. Where there is overlap, both teachers assess the projects together. No matter whether the library is on a fixed or flex schedule, at the end of the project all the teachers sit down, debrief, and reflect on what changes they may want or need to make next year's unit.

With all these examples, the learning is conceptually connected for the kids. There was a reason for what they were learning. It gave them a deep connection and better understanding of the biome and pond animals. Units like this one require someone to start the idea and take the lead. The school librarian is the perfect connector for bringing everyone together. Units like this can also lead to help convince administrators to look at a more flexible schedule model for the library.

Getting Started with Collaboration

To collaborate, you have to build trust between the collaborators. Classroom teachers must feel that they can trust the school librarian to deliver on what they promise. Collaboration tends to begin with small one-time lessons. Rarely does one jump right in with a multiday, multilayered project. It takes time to build those relationships to where teachers feel comfortable working with the school librarian on the bigger projects.

The beginning of collaboration often feels like a one-way street. The school librarian must take the initiative in promoting ideas and projects. The school librarian has to be asking questions:

- Which topics and concepts are coming up?

- In which areas could we use more resources on in the school library and in the classroom?

- How can I support what you are teaching in the classroom?

- How can we work together to design a project?

- I had an idea, what do you think of this?

- How can I help you integrate technology?

These questions might be asked while passing a teacher in the hallway, while eating lunch in the cafeteria, while a teacher has his or her class checking out books in the school library, while teachers are sitting down and planning, while teachers are meeting to develop long-term plans and curriculum, or even sent over the school e-mail.

Attitude is important during these discussions. There are teachers who don't like the ideas presented, don't want to work with the school librarian, or have a cavalier attitude about the whole thing. While that may be the attitude of the teacher, for the sake of the students the school librarian must persevere. Continue to offer ideas and suggestions. Continue to communicate with teachers (even with those who don't seem as interested). Continue to make it known that the school librarian is there and wants to be a partner. It may take some time, but even the most reluctant teachers will eventually come around. The pressure from seeing what their peers are doing is a great way to open up reluctant teachers to collaboration.

Administrators who see the benefits of collaboration may also help encourage reluctant teachers to work with the school library. A little encouragement from an administrator can go a long way to get even the most reticent teacher to want to collaborate with the library. There is a fine line between encouragement and mandate and the school librarian doesn't want to work with someone who is being forced, but a gentle nudge or mention from the administration might help move a teacher in the right direction.

When starting a new job (or even a new school year), the school librarian should ask to sit down with each grade level either during their prep or after school. Get administrative support by inviting them to these meetings. Be prepared ahead of time with an agenda (see Figure 4.2 for an example of a possible agenda) with one or two major topics for discussion. Use this time to make introductions, share the concept of collaborative planning, and provide some examples. Allow teachers to give feedback (be prepared that not everything they say will be music to the school librarian's ears). Try to develop a way to work with their concerns or suggestions. Ask them about one thing they liked best about the school library program and one thing they wish they could change. Take notes and share them with the grade level and administrators. These introductions can be a successful beginning to open a dialogue. The school library program is not all about the school librarian but rather all about student learning. Input from others helps the librarian to focus on his or her mission of helping students succeed.

In the years that follow, there may not be a need to do formal meetings with every teacher every summer. However, the school librarian may want to make sure to do this with new teachers every year. It is easier to present some of this information in small groups rather than a staff meeting. Staff meetings can feel like it is the school librarian versus the world. Small groups make it a more personal and manageable. Professional Learning Communities (PLCs) are another great way to meet with teachers in small groups. It allows you to focus the conversation on the issues and concerns of the small group, rather than those of the entire faculty at once.

As staff retires or teachers move to other grade levels, it may be good to have these meetings again to open up conversations. When new people enter the mix, opinions and ideas change, so it is always good to make sure the school librarian is aware of what is happening in the building.

Next, determine how the teachers plan their lessons each week. Here are some possible scenarios:

◆ Teacher plans on his or her own

◆ Teacher plans on his or her own but has a grade level curriculum map to guide them

◆ Teachers plan together as a grade level and have a grade level curriculum map to guide them

◆ Teachers plan as a grade level team along with other teachers (special education, library media, etc.)

The school librarian needs a copy of the grade-level curriculum maps or unit plans. These documents tend to be in a constant state of flux, so at the beginning of each year, ask for the current edition (if the school librarian wasn't part of the planning). Keep them in a binder

Collaboration Days
V. P. Barnes Elementary Library
Summer/Back to School

Outcomes:

- To begin to work together.
- To begin a long-term plan for collaboration.

Flexible Agenda:

Introductions
1. Name, grade level
2. What is your favorite children's author/book?

Something Old; Something New
- What do you like best about the library?
- If you could change one thing about the library, what would it be?

Long-Term Planning
- Calendar—Rough timeline for what themes/units you use to teach?
- Collection development—In which areas do we need more resources?

Resources:
- Academic standards
- Standards for 21st-century learner
- District curriculum/benchmarks
- Media/technology benchmarks
- Software/technology available

Figure 4.2   Agenda.

(or saved to the computer) for easy reference. Some districts also post their curriculum on the district webpage or adopt the statewide curriculum. Whether they are online or in print, the school librarian needs to have them and use them. These can not only help guide development of collaborative projects but they also give valuable information to assist with collection development. These guides may be the only standards to be covered or a scope and sequence, but teachers may take those and develop themes and units in a yearlong plan.

If teachers plan alone, using those yearlong planning guides will be important. The school librarian will need to utilize e-mail and face-to-face conversations to begin collaborating with teachers. If teachers plan together as a grade level team, ask them when they meet and plan to join them. Some teams will plan during their prep, some will plan before school, and some will plan after school. See Figure 4.3 for a sample of a weekly planning schedule. Keep in mind there is one school librarian and anywhere from five to seven or more grade levels depending on the configuration of the school. When beginning to collaborate, pick one or two grade levels to focus on making connections. Attend those planning sessions as frequently as possible. It may be impossible to attend every planning session, every week. But, certainly the school librarian should strive for that goal. The more information the school librarian has the easier it is to make connections. When the school librarian is unable to attend the planning meetings, let the teachers know and ask beforehand if there is anything you can do to help.

As time progresses, the school librarian can move to focus on other grade levels and spend more time at their planning sessions. This does not mean the school librarian stops going to the meetings of the other grade levels or that the school librarian drops the project and lessons they've planned in the past. However, once the school librarian has built a good relationship with one grade level, he or she can now spend a little less time with that grade level and a little more time with a grade level that he or she has not worked with before.

It is important to be a part of those planning discussions as much as possible, but reality says it will be almost impossible to get to every grade level every week. When grade levels plan during their preparation time, it can be really difficult. If the school librarian cannot attend their planning sessions, ask teachers to copy their plans or send a quick summary of the plan (either in paper or electronically). A short e-mail or a quick conversation before or after school can also be a good way to find out what teachers are doing in their classrooms. Make sure to stress that the school librarian needs to know what is happening and can make connections in the school library and to offer ideas, resources, and project possibilities.

Sustaining Collaboration

Once the door to collaboration is open, the real fun begins. One of the most frequent comments about why people enjoy working in the school library is because no two days are ever the same. Even projects that were developed several years ago need tweaked and altered to improve and make them better each year. They also need to be examined to ensure they are still matching with the curriculum requirements. Also, each year a new group of students is before the school librarian. The project may need alteration based on their prior knowledge, skills, or background.

	Monday	Tuesday	Wednesday	Thursday	Friday
Before School	4th Grade	3rd Grade			
During Prep				2nd Grade	
After School		1st Grade	Kindergarten		

It is helpful when each grade level plans at a different time. Unfortunately, that is not always feasible or something the school librarian can control. In cases like this, alternate from week to week or split your time in half for each grade level.

Figure 4.3 Weekly Planner.

The collaboration log helps to sustain collaboration because the school librarian has documentation from the previous year. He or she can review the log and keep up with teachers, "Hey, I noticed last year around this time we started project X. Would you like to schedule that again?" Documenting in a collaboration log helps the school librarian and teacher. It tracks and organizes the entire project. The log could be a simple GoogleForm to complete after each project, or keep a binder (or online copies) of Figure 4.4. Organize it chronologically in order to easily refer to it in future.

Attach any other handouts, notes, or materials created for the project.

Continuing to attend the grade-level planning meetings is also important. This constant contact keeps things from being lost in the shuffle. Teachers get busy and sometimes will forget or alter what they are doing each year. Changes in standards, new teachers, and a host of variables can cause changes from year to year. Being present at those meetings provides a reminder of the possibilities and the opportunities available in the school library.

Praise teachers who have done successful projects with the school librarian. Especially at the beginning, the teachers may feel like they are taking a risk when working with the school librarian. Send an e-mail to the principal talking about the great project and carbon copy the teacher so they can see the school librarian is bragging about them. In the library, newsletter highlights those teachers who are working with students in the school library this month. This not only gives a pat on the back to the teachers who were collaborating but it may just get some of those who are a little resistant to jump on the bandwagon.

Both beginning and maintaining collaboration requires administrative support. Make sure to keep the administrator in the loop about implementing a collaboration model. Show him or her samples of the lessons and projects so he or she can see the results of the effort. Once administrators are on board, they can help push the school even more down the collaborative road. They can ask teachers what they have been doing in the school library. They can encourage the collaborative connections. Their influence can go a long way to help build the collaborative environment. In addition, at some point the principal has to observe the teacher and the librarian, so it might be a great time during a collaborative project to invite the administrator. He or she can see the power of the collaboration and conduct an evaluation at the same time.

One day a principal was giving a tour of the school to a principal from another district. The principal shared about the collaborative environment at the school and how the school library program was an active part of it. He talked about how everything was planned as a team. The visiting principal asked, "How does the school librarian get the teachers to work with her?" The principal respond, "Well, she doesn't really give us a choice." At first thought, one might think that isn't really collaboration, but in reality that school librarian had been persistent to the point where she had wiggled her way into the grade levels and now it is just part of how the school operates. It wasn't a choice, but rather it was just a part of the learning culture in that school.

The school librarian's job is to teach and work with all students. It means that he or she has to work with all teachers in the building, too. It can be difficult when personalities clash, but the bottom line is serving the students. The school librarian and the teachers have to move past any possible differences they might have for the benefit of the students.

School Library Collaboration Planning & Teaching Log

Teacher(s): _____

Grade Level: _____   Planning Date: _____   Project Date:_____

Project Description/Timeline	Standards
	Teacher will:
School Improvement Goals Supported/Strategies Implemented	
Resources **Print:** **Databases:** **eBooks:** **Technology Tools:** **People:** **Other:**	**School Librarian will:**
Evaluation	

Figure 4.4   Sample Collaboration Form.

The proactive school librarian will move faster down the road to collaboration. The school librarian has to, at first, be the one who starts the collaboration discussions. It is unrealistic to think teachers will be breaking down the door to collaborate unless they have had previous experiences working with a good school librarian. The school librarian has to be the one to make that first step. However, once the door is open then other possibilities develop.

Documenting Collaboration

Keeping track of collaboration experiences is important for a couple of reasons. The first is to keep track of what role each participant in the project is playing. What is the teacher teaching? What is the school librarian teaching? Especially for first-time projects, making sure that everyone is on the same page is important. The second reason is that it provides proof of what the school library program offers at the school. The school librarian can track the number of classes, the number of projects, the number of students at each grade level. This can be important data to have available when discussing staffing, budgets, and schedules. The third reason is to provide a way to reflect on the project for future years. Having documentation can help when one goes to the next year to make the project even better (Loertscher 2000, pp. 81–84).

Figure 4.4 is a sample collaboration form. This collaboration log is based on the American Association of School Librarians' *Standards for the 21st Century Learner.* The traditional method would be to keep a binder where one would organize the forms based on the school calendar. Behind each form, one would include all the forms, handouts, notes, and resources for easy access. However, besides paper and pencil forms, consider electronic methods for collecting and organizing collaboration logs.

- ✦ Use a database program to create fields where data from the collaboration log can be entered.
- ✦ Use Excel to create a simple spreadsheet of data about each collaborative experience.
- ✦ Use Word to document each project. Create a document for each grade level or teacher and then just add to the list throughout the year.
- ✦ Use a Google Doc for the teacher and librarian to track things together.
- ✦ Create a Google Form to fill out to keep the data organized.
- ✦ Use a folder on the computer to keep all the related files. Organize all the projects into folders for each grade level.

These documents and records can be invaluable. Sometimes a teacher will come and say, "Remember that project we did three years ago?" With the collaboration log, one has the data and information to say, "Why, yes I do. Here is what was successful and here is where the school librarian can make some improvements. Want to try it again?" See Chapter 8 for more ideas and thoughts about why collecting data about collaborations is important.

Beyond the log, the school librarian can begin to map out what the year looks like. See Figure 4.5 for a sample yearlong planning form. The librarian can begin to see when major projects are happening, making sure to balance time (there are limits to how many major projects one can do at a time), and see where there are grade levels that need additional collaborative projects. (See Figures 4.6 and 4.7 for examples of documented collaboration projects.)

Month:				
	Week 1	Week 2	Week 3	Week 4
Kindergarten	Topics/Unit Themes			
1st Grade				
2nd Grade				
3rd Grade				
4th Grade				
Special Areas, Special Education, and FOCUS				

Figure 4.5   Yearlong Plan.

School Library
Collaboration Planning and Teaching Log

Teacher(s): _____

Grade Level: ___Primary Grades_____   Planning Date: _____   Project Date:_____

Standards for 21st-Century Learner	Project Description
1 Inquire, think critically, and gain knowledge. a. Skills: __1.1.1, 1.1.3, 1.1.4, 1.1.6___ b. Dispositions: __1.2.1, 1.2.6_____ c. Responsibilities: __1.3.1, 1.3.5____ d. Self-assessment: __1.4.1, 1.4.4___ **2 Draw conclusions, make informed decisions, apply knowledge to new situations, and create new knowledge.** a. Skills: ____2.1.1, 2.1.3_____ b. Dispositions: _____ c. Responsibilities: _____ d. Self-assessment: _____ **3 Share knowledge and participate ethically and productively as members of our democratic society.** a. Skills: ___3.1.3_____ b. Dispositions: _____ c. Responsibilities: _____ d. Self-assessment: _____ **4 Pursue personal and aesthetic growth.** a. Skills: _____ b. Dispositions: _____ c. Responsibilities: _____ d. Self-assessment: _____	✦ Students will choose an animal from the pond biome. Students will follow the Big6 using a research journal to track and organize their research. ✦ They will brainstorm a list of questions to locate about their animal. ✦ Students will then have to determine if that animal could live in the rain forest, too. They have to prove their answer based on the facts they found. The evidence must support their answer that they choose. ✦ Students will create a short video commercial about their animal and share why or why it couldn't live in the rain forest. Timeline: ✦ 2 to 3 visits to the LMC for research. ✦ A couple of days to a week in the classroom to use their research to determine if their animal could live in the rain forest and then write the report with evidence along with the script for the commercial. ✦ They will also need some time in the video studio to put their commercial together.
Academic Standards English/Language Arts Writing	**Teacher will:** ✦ Introduce the biomes in the classroom prior to starting the project. ✦ Assist students while they are using the library resources. ✦ Assess the final product.
School Improvement **Goals Supported/Strategies Implemented** Literacy—providing proof for answers	

Resources			School librarian will:
X Online Resources	Video Production	Streaming Video	✦ Guide the students through the Big6 process in locating the information for their projects. ✦ Assist students while they are using the library resources. ✦ Assess the research journals students use to track their research process.
PowerPoint	Multimedia Software	Scanner	
Word	Inspiration / Kidspiration **X**	Other: Books Other:	
Excel	Digital Cameras **X**	Encyclopedia	
Blog / Wiki **X**	Digital Video Cameras	Other:	

Evaluation

Teacher and school librarian will take time to debrief the project and adjust as needed for next year.

Source: Collaboration Log © 2008, Carl A. Harvey II—http://www.carl-harvey.com.

Excerpted from *Standards for the 21st-Century Learner* by the American Association of School Librarians, a division of the American Library Association, copyright © 2007 American Library Association. Available for download at www.ala.org/aasl/standards. Used with permission.

Figure 4.6 Sample Collaborative Lesson.

School Library
Collaboration Planning and Teaching Log

Teacher(s): _____

Grade Level: __Intermediate Grades_____ Planning Date: _____ Project Date:_____

Standards for 21st-Century Learner	Project Description
5. Inquire, think critically, and gain knowledge. a. Skills: _1.1.1, 1.1.4, 1.1.3, 1.1.8____ b. Dispositions: __1.2.1_____ c. Responsibilities: __1.3.1, 1.3.5_____ d. Self-assessment: ____1.4.2_____ **6. Draw conclusions, make informed decisions, apply knowledge to new situations, and create new knowledge.** a. Skills: __2.1.2, 2.1.4_____ b. Dispositions: _____ c. Responsibilities: __2.3.1_____ d. Self-assessment: __2.4.1_____ **7. Share knowledge and participate ethically and productively as members of our democratic society.** a. Skills: __3.1.1, 3.1.3_____ b. Dispositions: _____3.2.3_____ c. Responsibilities: __3.3.4_____ d. Self-assessment: __3.4.2_____ **8. Pursue personal and aesthetic growth.** a. Skills: _____ b. Dispositions: _____ c. Responsibilities: _____ d. Self-assessment: _____	✦ Students are going to an overnight trip to the state capitol. They are responsible for planning all the details of the trip. ✦ Students will brainstorm what task needs to be completed to be ready for the trip. Understanding, more may be added as time goes on to the list. ✦ They have to provide choices for travel, lodging, activities, meals, and so on. Justification will be important, and the class (along with the teacher's guidance) will make the final choices. Timeline: ✦ Students will spend a day brainstorming tasks to complete. ✦ Students will work on search strategies to locate the need information. They'll need a couple of visits at least to locate what they need. ✦ Students will create a presentation to the class about what they found, so decisions can be made.

Academic Standards	Teacher will:
Math and Social Studies	✦ The teacher will provide background knowledge and help the students brainstorm the list of tasks to complete. ✦ Provide support to the students with their research. ✦ Co-assess the video and research materials with school librarian.
School Improvement Goals Supported/Strategies Implemented Mathematics	

Resources			School Librarian will:
X Online Resources	Video Production	Streaming Video	✦ Guide the students through the Big6 to research the information they need. ✦ Help guide them on web searches to learn how to find what they need efficiently and effectively. ✦ Co-assess the video and research materials.
___ PowerPoint	Multimedia Software	Scanner	
___ Word	Inspiration / Kidspiration **X**	Other: Books Other:	
___ Excel	Digital Cameras **X**	Encyclopedia	
___ Blog / Wiki **X**	Digital Video Cameras	Other:	

Evaluation

Teacher and school librarian will take time to debrief the project and adjust as needed for next year.

Source: Collaboration Log © 2008, Carl A. Harvey II—http://www.carl-harvey.com.

Excerpted from *Standards for the 21st-Century Learner* by the American Association of School Librarians, a division of the American Library Association, copyright © 2007 American Library Association. Available for download at www.ala.org/aasl/standards. Used with permission.

Figure 4.7 Sample Collaborative Lesson.

Beyond the Core Content

School librarians often work with the core-content subjects such as language arts, math, social studies, and science. School librarians gravitate to these subjects because they are what are taught in the classroom, and they are what gets tested. The resources in the school library are heavily focused on the content standards and subjects. However, what about the other subjects that are taught in the school?

Related Arts

Related arts could include art, music, physical education, counselors, foreign language, technology, or any subject that is in the rotation that provides teacher release time. Often the school library program is also included in these related arts if the library is on a fixed schedule. The related arts teachers can often be a good place to collaborate.

Consider the music class that is studying composers. Students could research a composer and then create a game based on the information they found to teach the other students in their class about the composer. Student must create a game from scratch. They can base it on Monopoly or CandyLand or any type of board game that students can play. The game focuses on determining why the composer was important and by the end of the game all the participants should know the composer's contribution.

On a flexible schedule, the school librarian could attend music class to work with students, or on a fixed schedule, the project could be scheduled so students research their composers during both their music and their library special time. Related arts teachers who experience the benefits of a flexible schedule school library program can become staunch advocates for keeping the school librarian out of the rotation. One librarian was kept from being in the specials rotation because the music teacher was able to demand how much they needed the librarian for her projects and classes. Reaching out the hand to offer help and collaboration can build a bridge that creates an ardent supporter of the school library program.

Special Education

Differentiating instruction is a challenging goal. Special education teachers are experts at taking grade level content and presenting it to students at the appropriate level of difficulty. For example, one day the school librarian suggested doing a research project with the special needs students in a particular grade level. The content taught was the same as the classroom content, but the resources and final product were modified to meet the students' needs. Once the project was over, the special education teacher commented that in all her years of teaching she had never had a school librarian offer to work with her kids. She loved it. Now the team regularly plans together for other opportunities for the students to work in the school library.

As a school librarian builds a collection, there is always focus on trying to find several resources at multiple reading levels. It would seems an obvious connection to work with the special education teachers to make sure they know these resources are available and to take that one step further and plan lesson and projects.

School librarians cannot focus exclusively on the general classroom teacher. The school librarian has a responsibility to related arts and special education, too. The AASL standards apply to all subjects and all students. It is good for students to see those connections outside the core standards.

One thing that is important about school libraries is they have always been a place where anyone can learn. School librarian needs to be aware of how students are identified, what support resources need to be available to them, and determine by working with the special education teachers how the school library program can have an impact for all students in the building.

English Language Learner (ELL)

ELLs are also another population growing in many schools across the country. ELL students are those who need additional language support. Perhaps they moved to this country and do not know English, or perhaps English is not spoken at home, so they need additional practice and support. The school library can be another place for these students to feel a part of the school. It can be a place where they feel they are successful and included.

It will be important to work with the ELL teachers to determine how the school library program can be supportive. The school library might need to expand its collection of bilingual resources to support struggling ELL readers. The school librarian may need to help classroom teachers adapt and modify projects for ELL students. Materials at a variety of levels on a variety of topics will be important so that ELL can be successful while working in the school library, too.

Either special education or ELL requires the school librarian to be aware of the students in his or her building. They need to talk with teachers about the needs and issues the children they are working with have. This will allow the school librarian to better focus on working with those children and meeting their needs.

Instruction Organization

As collaboration becomes the norm in the school, develop a yearlong plan for the school library to map out the units and instruction. Use the collaboration log to help develop the plan so that it can include both big projects and those that have maybe just one or two lessons. See Figure 4.5 for a sample chart. Use a spreadsheet, document, a GoogleDoc to make it easy to update and change as the year progresses. It can also help the school librarian to track busier times of the year. The school librarian may want to try and stagger bigger projects so multiple grade level are not all involved in mega projects all at once. Also consider the gradual release of responsibility. Just as teachers feel more comfortable with units and projects, they can take the lead so that the school librarian can focus on new projects and on new teachers who may need more support as they experience collaboration. The school librarian is still there to offer support and there are areas of projects like gathering or evaluating sources a librarian might always want to be a part of, but the teacher begins to take the lead. For example, one librarian spent a lot of time in teaching accessing online tools with computers. After a few years, the teacher felt comfortable doing that part, so the librarian could focus on another project.

The focus of this book is on the management side of school librarianship for elementary school libraries. So, this chapter focused heavily on knowing the standards, relationship building, and collaboration. The areas that are not focused as much in this book are specific instructional strategies or inquiry methods. Those are all topics covered in the further reading in more detail.

School librarians have seen their job evolve over the decades. The role school librarian play with curriculum—planning, teaching and assessing—has grown dramatically. School librarians play a pivotal role in preparing students for the 21st century.

Works Cited

American Association of School Librarians. *Empowering Learners: Guidelines for School Library Programs*. Chicago, IL: American Association of School Librarians, 2009.

American Association of School Librarians. *Standards for the 21st Century Learner in Action*. Chicago, IL: American Association of School Librarians, 2009.

Buzzeo, Toni. *The Collaboration Handbook*. Columbus, OH: Linworth Publishing, Inc., 2008.

Buzzeo, Toni. "Collaborating from the Center of the School Universe." *Library Media Connection*, 24, no. 4 (January 2006): 18–21.

Harada, Violet H., and Joan M. Yoshina. *Assessing Learning: Librarians and Teachers as Partners*. Westport, CT: Libraries Unlimited, 2005.

Loertscher, David V. *Taxonomies of the School Library Program*, 2nd edition. San Jose, CA: Hi Willow Research and Publishing, 2000.

Further Reading

Calkins, Lucy, Mary Ehrenworth, and Christopher Lehman. *Pathways to the Common Core: Accelerating Achievement*. Portsmouth, NH: Heinemann Educational Books, 2012.

Callison, Daniel J. *The Evolution of Inquiry: Controlled, Guided, Modeled, and Free*. Santa Barbara, CA: Libraries Unlimited, 2015.

Callison, Daniel J., and Leslie B. Preddy. *The Blue Book on Information Age Inquiry, Instruction, and Literacy*. Santa Barbara, CA: Libraries Unlimited, 2006.

Crane, Beverley E. *How to Teach: A Practical Guide for Librarians*. Lanham, MA: Rowman & Littlefield Publishers, 2013.

Harada, Violet H., and Sharon Coatney, eds. *Inquiry and the Common Core: Librarians and Teachers Designing Teaching for Learning*. Santa Barbara, CA: Libraries Unlimited, 2013.

Harvey, Carl A., II, and Linda L. Mills. *Leading the Common Core Initiative: A Guide for K-5 School Librarians*. Santa Barbara, CA: Libraries Unlimited, 2015.

Kuhlthau, Carol Collier, Leslie K. Maniotes, and Ann K. Caspari. *Guided Inquiry: Learning in the 21st Century*. Santa Barbara, CA: Libraries Unlimited, 2015.

Lamb, Annette. "Information Instruction: Strategies for Library and Information Professionals." Accessed February 27, 2016. http://eduscapes.com/instruction/index.htm.

Ratzer, Mary Boyd, and Paige Jaeger. *Rx for the Common Core: Toolkit for Implementing Inquiry Learning*. Santa Barbara, CA: Libraries Unlimited, 2014.

Ratzer, Mary Boyd, and Paige Jaeger. *Think Tank Library: Brain-Based Learning Plans for New Standards, Grades K-5*. Santa Barbara, CA: Libraries Unlimited, 2014.

Ratzer, Mary Boyd, and Paige Jaeger. *Think Tank Library: Brain-Based Learning Plans for New Standards, Grades 6–12*. Santa Barbara, CA: Libraries Unlimited, 2015.

Reeves, Anne R. *Where Great Teaching Begins: Planning for Student Thinking and Learning*. Alexandria, VA: Association for Supervision & Curriculum Development, 2011.

Small, Ruth V., Marylin P. Arnone, and Barbara K. Stripling. *Teaching for Inquiry: Engaging the Learner Within*. New York: Neal-Schuman Publishers, 2011.

Stripling, Barbara K., and Sandra Hughes-Hassell, eds. *Curriculum Connections through the Library*. Westport, CT: Libraries Unlimited, 2003.

Turner, Philip M., and Ann Marlow Riedling. *Helping Teachers Teach: A School Library Media Specialist's Role*, 3rd edition. Westport, CT: Libraries Unlimited, 2003.

Wiggins, Grant P., and Jay McTighe. *Understanding by Design*. Alexandria, VA: Association for Supervision and Curriculum Development, 1998.

Zmuda, Allison, Violet H. Harada, and Grant Wiggins. *Librarians as Learning Specialists: Meeting the Learning Imperative for the 21st Century*. Santa Barbara, CA: Libraries Unlimited, 2008.

CHAPTER 5

Programming

The library is the largest instructional space within the school. The librarian works to create not only an attractive, warm, and inviting physical space, but also a culture of welcome and acceptance.

> — Audrey P. Church, *Tapping into the Skills of the 21st Century School Librarians: A Concise Handbook for Administrators*

Beyond instruction, the school library program also offers programming to students and staff. The school librarian designs programming to motivate students to read, to interact with technology, and to come to the school library. These additional connections can create lasting memories for students that give them a positive feeling about the school library. Programs are also some of the ways to get word out into the community about the positive happenings in the school library.

Curricular Connections

There are so many options about what programming could be happening in the library before, during, and after school. At the same time, there is usually just one school librarian (and maybe some support staff), so there is the factor of time and energies to focus on programming. The primary mission of a school library is to impact student learning. Therefore, it is important while determining what type of programming the library might offer that the connection to the curriculum and instruction be on top of the list of factors to consider.

At the same time, there may be interesting programming ideas that pique student interest and encourage lifelong learning. Creating that love of learning and peaking students' interest is also the key to a successful school library program. The key is to make sure that the programming in the school library is above and beyond the instruction happening. It is important to make sure everything has a purpose.

Community Connections

It is always great to branch out beyond the walls of the school library. Bringing in the community is a great way to build support for the school and the school library program and, more important, connect students to the world around them. Are there guest speakers who connect to a project or unit a teacher is doing? Are there community leaders who can demonstrate what their role is in making their local community function? Are there businesses that could have connections? The school library, as the information source for the school, would be a great way to facilitate and build those community relationships.

In one school, the librarian was in charge of making connections for enrichment programs. As part of that job, the librarian made sure to connect with business leaders and community members. When there were appropriate opportunities to invite them into the school to present or work with students, the school librarian was the primary person who made the connection between the community and the classroom.

Public Library

Programming is an opportunity to make connections with the public library. They offer many programs for elementary age students. The school library can promote those events. Hang up flyers, invite the public librarians in to talk about the programs, or just include information in the school newsletter or school library website. At the same time, there may be opportunities to plan programming together. Could the school librarian and public librarian work together to bring in an author? Could the school and public librarians organize a student presentation at the public library to share their research? There are many opportunities to work together, and it builds an advocacy network for both types of libraries.

Promoting Reading

No doubt one of the elements that most school librarians love is the promotion of reading. School librarians love to share and talk about books. School librarians know that reading helps students grow and learn.

Reader Advisory

This seems obvious, but the best way to encourage reading is to talk about great books with students (and staff). As new material comes in, as students share their interest, this is a great time to point them to what the school library has to offer. When the school librarian makes that one-on-one connection with a student and the right book, it is just magical.

Look for ways to free up the school librarian from being tied to the circulation desk during check out. If there is a library aide, that helps to free up the librarian to be circulating among the students. If it is a flexible schedule, the classroom teacher can run the circulation system while the librarian is out with the students (most systems are pretty simple for all types of users). Finally, one of the easiest ways to free up personnel from the circulation desk (often the adults need to be out helping students find books instead of from behind the desk) is to move to a self-checkout system. Most automation systems allow you to print student barcodes, which can be used to make library cards. From the beginning of the year, teach students to scan their cards, items, and then sometimes there is a command barcode that can be scanned to reset the screen for the next students. It's quick, efficient, and frees up staff. An alert can usually be put on the system if anything goes wrong. Odds are there is a chance something may not get checked out, but typically the books always come back and the amount of staff it frees up is HUGE!

Promotional Activities

There are all kinds of way to have fun in the library while promoting the library. In honor of Roald Dahl's 50th anniversary of *Charlie and the Chocolate Factory*, one librarian hid golden tickets in 10 of the books in the library. When students checked them out, they won a free copy of *Charlie and the Chocolate Factory*.

How about a reading contest where the class that reads the most pages/words gets to earn a reading party in the library? During certain months, highlight the authors and illustrators celebrating a birthday and celebrate their books.

If the school does a live morning announcement show, use that forum as a great opportunity to promote the library. One school scheduled book reviews, promoted library events, and even brought on students to share the projects they were working on in the library.

Contests for teachers are also a good idea. How about hiding a message in the library newsletter and offering a candy treat for whoever reads that part of the newsletter. It is always a great trick to get them to read the entire thing. For staff morale one year, one librarian hosted an Easter egg hunt throughout the library. It got them looking around at all the various resources while having some fun.

Reading Aloud

The traditional model of a story and check out for school libraries have been there for a long time. As school libraries have focused more on research, inquiry, and instruction, some of that story time opportunity has been lost. While school librarians certainly should be moving to higher-level activities, there can still be a place and time for sharing a great read aloud. Today's school librarian has to be more intentional about what they read aloud, why they are reading, and what connections it has to whatever project they are working on.

What is the purpose of the read aloud? There are often lots of great readers who don't have the specific training a school librarian does. When a school librarian is doing a read aloud, are there ways to maximize the learning of the students and skillset of the school librarian. There is a great opportunity for promotion of reading with read aloud. There is a great opportunity for modeling fluency and reading for understanding with a read aloud. There is a great opportunity for summarize and retelling with a read aloud. So, the opportunities are there, but school librarians need to take reading aloud to a whole new level.

Celebrations

Throughout the year, there are countless special events and days that can be celebrated in the library. Authors' birthdays, anniversaries of books published, and all sorts of other options. See Figure 5.1 for some possibilities. This can be a great way to have fun in the library while learning at the same time. Many of these events lend well to collaborations with other schools. Consider connecting with another school for World Read Aloud day and share stories with each other.

Policies

In Chapter 7, the book focuses on the importance of policies and procedures, but in this section it is clearly noted that the policies can have a huge impact on students' reading and promotion. Consider a library where students come once a week to check out materials, they are limited to two items, and they don't come back to the school library for another week. The student takes the books home and reads them that night, but they remain in his or her desk the rest of the week until it is time to go back to the library. Now, think about a school where students come to the school library and check out books. They can check out unlimited number; however, the librarian does discuss being responsible users. The student opts to check out three books. The student takes them home, reads them, and brings them back to school the next day when he or she can go to the library again for more. Now, which student is going to have more access to reading materials? How do policies impact the promotion of reading? Consider the policies in the school library now. What could be changed to increase student use and interest? Even in a fixed schedule environment, are there ways to increase student access to materials?

Young Author's Celebration

Celebrating student writing is important. In one school, annually students prepare one piece of writing that they take through the entire writing process all the way to publishing. This writing is then displayed and shared during a Young Author's Celebration. Students are encouraged to donate writing to the school library for others to read and enjoy as well.

Some school libraries have a special, appropriately decorated "author's chair" where students sign up with the school librarian to sit in the author's chair and read a work written by the student.

January	100 Days of School
February	Valentine's Day
	President's Day
	Black History Month
March	World Read Aloud Day
	Read Across America
April	Poem in Your Pocket Day
	School Library Month
	Drop Everything and Read—April 12
	El dia de los ninos/El dia de los—April 30
May	Children's Book Week
	Teacher Appreciation Week
	Asian Pacific American Heritage Month
June	Flag Day
	Reading over the Summer
July	Reading over the Summer
	4th of July
August	Welcome Back to School
September	Dot Day
	Library Card Sign-Up Month
	Hispanic Heritage Month
October	Read for the Record
November	Picture Book Month
	National Gaming Day
	American Indian, Alaska Native, and Native Hawaii Heritage Month
December	Melvil Dewey's Birthday
Various Times of Year	Ivy and Bean Day

Figure 5.1   Calendar of Events to Promote.

Moving beyond printing out these books, students could use a wiki or a website as a way to share their writing. Students could use digital storytelling tools and apps to create a story for sharing. Consider posting these to the Internet as well. The Internet and collaborative tools allow students to expand their audience for their writing. Imagine the joy of a grandparent in California who can hear and see their grandchild in Virginia reading a story he or she wrote. Be sure to follow district guidelines for posting student work online and comply with copyright guidelines.

Student Choice State Book Award Programs

Many states have a book award to honor authors and illustrators at various levels. These awards are often given based on the book that receives the most student votes. Committees of various groups (quite often school library or reading professional organizations) compile a list of nominees and then the students read them and vote on their favorite. Voting day can often be a huge celebration in the school library.

Planning is important to make sure the school library collection has the books available and a sufficient supply for readers to get access to them. Some libraries might make the picture book nominees a traveling cart that can go from room to room to be read. Some libraries might buy multiple copies of the chapter books. This is a good time for investing in some paperbacks to save some money and since the school library may not need five or six copies of this title years down the road.

The authors and illustrators love these awards because students vote on the winner. Most have stickers the school librarian can mark the books for easy access and to support the winner and nominees. State book awards are a great way to promote reading throughout the school.

Extracurricular Clubs
Book Clubs

There are many different types of book clubs. There are the traditional clubs where the students read the same book and come together at a set time to discuss it. There are clubs where all students read books by the same author. Again, they come together at a set time to discuss the books, themes, and style of the author. In elementary schools, lunchtime makes a great time to pull groups like this together where students can eat and discuss at the same time. Book clubs could be formal where everyone in the class is in some sort of club, or more informal where it is optional for the students.

Another option might be to look into a virtual book club. Maybe students meet via the school's learning management system to write and discuss the book they read. It could be that students set-up a blog or other form of communication tool in order to share their thoughts and ideas about books the club is reading. A virtual club could be a great way to meet up with students from another school and talk about the same book. Using tools such as Google Hangouts, FaceTime, and Skype gives the book club the opportunity to break out beyond the school walls. Connect with another school in the district, county, and state to have an amazing discussion. State book award nominees could be perfect for such an activity.

Another option for a book club is to bring parents and children together to read. Choose a book that appeals to many people on a variety of levels. Use some of the aforementioned technology options to interact, or perhaps a school-wide celebration for students and parents to share with each other about the book they read.

Student Assistant Club

Student assistants can provide invaluable help to the school library. They could be there to support the library or to help with technology. Some schools might call them by a clever name such as Jr. Librarians or the Clickers. Students might help with some of the clerical tasks in the school library and then they may also become experts on technology to help other students or teachers. See Chapter 2 for a potential list of tasks.

This club could meet before or after school, or students could come to the school library during recess. Have students apply for the positions at the beginning of the year. They need to fill out a simple application. See Figure 5.2 for an example of a possible application. One school has two slots each day where six students come to work in the school library. Students come only once a week. This way, they also get their recess most of the week. Their club can accommodate up to 60 students. A checklist keeps track of what job students have learned. This helps make it manageable for the library staff. See Figure 5.3 for a sample checklist.

Technology clubs are a great way to train small groups of students who can in turn support their teachers and fellow students. This club could be folded in with the student assistant club, or it could be a club on its own. Each class would have one or two representatives in the club. The club would focus on a variety of technology tools available in the building—from basic troubleshooting of a printer, changing toners, or assistance with using peripherals (digital cameras, iPads, scanners, etc.)

The student then becomes an expert, so if teachers have difficulties, the first call is to their student technology club member, and then if they still need help they can contact the school librarian or technology support people. This gives the kids some ownership and hopefully cuts down on the time a school librarian might spend solving some basic problems.

Morning Announcements

A lot of schools have access to equipment to do a morning announcements show over a closed circuit system. Some schools record it and some schools perform it live each day. Students take on the roles of anchors, producers, writers, reporters, directors, and teleprompters. The crew might be anywhere from 6 to 10 students. Some programs rotate their crew periodically to give more students an opportunity to be a part of the team.

Do you like to help out in the school?
Do you enjoy working with technology?
Do you like looking and working with all the
great books in the library media center?

If you answered yes, apply now to join the North
Library Media Center Clickers!

Name: _____

Teacher: _____

Why would you like to join the North Library Media Center Clickers?

What LifeSkills™ would you use if you were a member of the North Library Media Center Clickers?

Teacher's Signature_____

Figure 5.2 Student Helper Application.

	Turn-on Lights	Turn-on Computers	Writing Center	Research Journals	DIR Tickets Sort (Fri)	Dust/Clean	Trim Lamination	Die Cut Letters	Run Copies	Make Posters	Load Paper in Printers	Clean Computer Screens	Digital Cameras	Flip Video Cameras	Pull Books for Teachers	Checkin/Checkout Books	Straighten Shelves	Shelve—Enjoyable	Shelve—Fiction	Shelve—Non-Fiction	Shelve—Begin Chpt	Shelve—Graphic Novels	Shelve—Magazines	Shelve—Biographies	Shelve—Reference	Shelve—Videos	Shelve—Professional	Straighten Puppets
Monday—Lunch																												
Student Name—Room Number																												
Student Name—Room Number																												
Student Name—Room Number																												
Student Name—Room Number																												
Student Name—Room Number																												
Student Name—Room Number																												
Monday—Recess																												
Student Name—Room Number																												
Student Name—Room Number																												
Student Name—Room Number																												
Student Name—Room Number																												
Student Name—Room Number																												
Student Name—Room Number																												
Tuesday—Lunch																												
Student Name—Room Number																												
Student Name—Room Number																												
Student Name—Room Number																												
Student Name—Room Number																												
Student Name—Room Number																												
Student Name—Room Number																												
Tuesday—Recess																												
Student Name—Room Number																												
Student Name—Room Number																												
Student Name—Room Number																												
Student Name—Room Number																												
Student Name—Room Number																												
Student Name—Room Number																												

Figure 5.3 Student Helper Checklist.

Morning announcements are a great vehicle for students to practice public speaking, working on writing and editing, learning to use a variety of technology equipment, and a good opportunity to promote the school library program too.

Often the school librarian is in charge of the morning announcement, so as was mentioned earlier in the chapter, this would be a great forum for promoting what is happening in the library and the school. Consider recording the announcements and posting them online for families to see in the evening (make sure any parental permission is obtained and district policy is followed).

This could be a club that meets before or after school; it could be the team meets for a few minutes each morning to practice before going live. It could be that a training session is offered on the equipment to cut down on the time away from class to produce the morning announcements. One librarian hosted a summer workshop each year where her students came in and really got time to practice and learning the equipment. When they started the school year, the focus on was on preparing each day and not learning the equipment.

The crew could help expand their role to utilize the studio beyond the morning announcements. Students who have been on the crew can be experts when their classes are using the studio for projects.

Enrichments and Special Programs

The school library program has the opportunity and often the space to plan and host wonderful enrichment programs for students. One school librarian was put in charge of enrichments for the school by the PTO and given an annual budget. This was the springboard to making enrichment programs that connected to the curriculum and supported activities in the library too!

Author Visits

Author visits are a real-life experience for students and staff. To connect with the authors and illustrators who write the books that line the shelves is a thrill they will remember long after they leave the halls of the school. A typical author visit provides for one to three convocations during the day. The author will also have a book signing session where students and staff can get their books autographed. These events become ingrained in the students' memories. Circulation of the visiting author's books remains high for many years after the visit.

It creates a shared experience for the entire school. Whenever possible host an author in the school library. It is a more intimate setting. One library moves out all of the furniture to make room for entire grade levels to sit on the floor to listen to the author's speech.

Bringing authors to the school is an investment. The costs of an author visit can be quite large depending on the author's speaking fees, transportation, and lodging. If not pulling in a local author, a good budget to start with is $2,000 but know that the price can vary greatly. This is a great opportunity to work with the PTA/PTO to secure funding or to write a grant. Consider using book fair funds as a means of supporting the author visit. Maybe there are other ideas for a fund-raiser that might benefit bringing in an author. See if there are other schools in the area that would like to split the travel costs as a means for saving money. In addition, most author visits include selling the author's books to students and staff who would like to get the books autographed. Most publishers (if you order directly from them) or local bookstore offer a discount of 20–40 percent. If the library sells them at full price, there is some profit that could be used to start the fund for the next visit. Be creative in trying to secure the funds. The benefits to students far outweigh the costs.

Preparing the students ahead of time is the key. Make sure they are well versed in the author's books. In addition, they want to make sure to have learned about the author. Where is he or she from? What inspires him or her? Students need to make a connection, and by prepping them ahead of time it makes the experience that more meaningful. Purchase additional copies of the book for the collection. They will keep being checked out long after the visit.

So, how can school librarian use technology to bring authors into the schools? Many authors now offer a chance to connect virtually with them. While these may not be free, the fees might be less expensive than bringing the author to the school to visit face to face. There are many tools such as Skype, Google Hangouts, and FaceTime that provide a format for connecting electronically with minimal technology costs. Just as with the face-to-face visit, the prep ahead of time will be important. Students should still be well versed with the books and the author before connecting. While the opportunity for autographs and getting books might not be there as there would be in a face-to-face visit, there is still a lot of meaningful conversation that can be had connecting with an author online.

After-School Programs

Bring students into the school library after school to celebrate reading. At one school, an after-school program is a way to motivate students to read books off the state student choice award. All students read the same book and then stay after school for a program where there are activities based on the book they read.

Beyond the school day the school library can also offer support for tutoring. Look for opportunities for funding to keep the school library open after school (or before school) for tutoring. Can you get volunteers or teachers to help offer support for students? It will be important to make sure transportation is also available for students who stay late whether that be provided by the school district or whether parents need to make other arrangements.

What about when students are in the middle of big projects? Can the school library be opened in the evenings for parents and students to use? Can grant funds be found to pay for staff to stay and keep the facility available in the evening? Is there a way to adjust hours of support staff to cover evening hours? The school librarian needs to work with administrators to look for creative ways to fund and offer services to students.

Makerspaces

Leslie Preddy in her book *School Library Makerspaces* defines makerspaces as "a community destination where students—sometimes alongside staff, parents, and mentors—can create, problem solve, and develop skills, talents, thinking, and mental rigor" (Preddy 2013, p. 1). The wonderful thing about a makerspace is that each library can truly adapt and alter them based on the resources and space they have available.

There are all types of ways to utilize a makerspace. Options could be available for students to work on after they have finished checking out. Students can also access it during recess, or the librarian might decide to have a before- or after-school club. Finally, and more important, students could integrate these projects into what they are doing in the classroom. The options are truly endless.

Funding for the makerspace may be different as typically library budget are already stretched. However, makerspaces are great because they use a variety of tools, supplies, and materials that people often have at home. Consider a drive asking families to donate things for the makerspace. The community and school families may be happy to take some time to clear out old crafting supplies or materials that will be perfect for a makerspace. Because of the creativity and curiosity makerspaces foster, they would be a great focus for grant funds as well. It may be good to target families at the high school or community with grown children. They may have old toys or LEGOS that they'd like to part with to add to the library makerspace.

Not only is funding a stretch but it is also a stretch to find the space in a library. One librarian cleaned out an office and used it to store the supplies and projects until students needed or wanted to work on them. Other libraries have cleared off some shelves and use those to organize their makerspace supplies.

There are all kind of opportunities and resources for using a makerspace. They are a great way to bring in the community. Consider how experts at recycling could come in and talk about repurposing materials instead of using them in a landfill. Makerspaces are great for involving parents. Consider hosting family nights where parents and students can create and explore in the makerspace.

It really is just another type of collection the library is providing and a way for students to share and explore what they are learning at the same time.

Gaming

Gaming in libraries has been another hook to bring students into the school library. From board games to electronic games, libraries are offering programming. Christopher Harris and the member librarians of the Genesee Valley BOCES in New York have created an alignment of gaming with the *Standards for the 21st Century Learner*. Check out their website for the alignment and other gaming resources: sls.gvboces.org/gaming/.

Gaming could be special events offered after school or even a lunchtime/recess activity. Many of the games have curricular connections that could be resources for literacy or math stations in the classroom. Gaming is an example of how 21st-century libraries are pulling in students by going to where the students are interested.

Coding

Another option for students to be creative is coding. The Hour of Code, https://hourofcode.com, is a great resource for ideas for supporting and creating coders in the school library. This program focuses on how anyone can learn coding language to promote computer sciences. The librarian might offer this as part of the makerspace activities, maybe a separate club, or maybe a special event to promote in the school. Coding is just another way to support exploration and creativity in the library.

Years after they leave the school, students are not going to remember a worksheet they filled out or a test they took. Create those learning opportunities that are unique and meaningful and students will remember them for a lifetime. They'll have a positive response anytime someone begins to talk about school libraries.

Work Cited

Preddy, Leslie B. *School Library Makerspaces: Grades 6–12*. Santa Barbara, CA: Libraries Unlimited, 2013.

Further Reading

Adams, Suellen S. *Crash Course in Gaming*. Santa Barbara, CA: Libraries Unlimited, 2014.

American Association of School Librarians. *Standards for the 21st Century Learner*. Chicago, IL: American Association of School Librarians, 2007.

Freeman, Judy, and Caroline Feller Bauer. *The Handbook for Storytellers*. Chicago, IL: ALA Editions, 2015.

Freeman, Judy, and Caroline Feller Bauer. *The Handbook for Storytime Programs*. Chicago, IL: ALA Editions, 2015.

Harvey, Carl A., II. "Authors + Students = A Powerful Special Event." *Library Media Connection* 31, no. 5 (March/April 2013): 48.

Harvey, Carl A., II. "Bringing Authors to Students." *School Library Media Activities Monthly* 22, no. 4 (December 2005): 28–30.

Marks, Diana F. *The Big Book of Glues, Brews, and Goos: 500+ Kid-Tested Recipes and Formulas for Hands-On Learning*. Santa Barbara, CA: Libraries Unlimited, 2014.

Mayer, Brian, and Christopher Harris. *Libraries Got Game: Aligned Learning through Modern Board Games*. Chicago, IL: American Library Association, 2010.

McGhee, Marla W., and Barbara A. Jansen. *The Principal's Guide to a Powerful Library Media Program*, 2nd edition. Santa Barbara, CA: Linworth Publishing, 2010.

Miller, Donalyn. *The Book Whisperer: Awakening the Inner Reader in Every Child*. San Francisco, CA: Wiley, John & Sons, 2009.

Patterson, Penny. "Maker Assistants Make Maker Nights Happen." *School Library Connection* 1, no. 3 (November 2015): 20–21.

Schnell, Agee. "You Too Can Host an Author/Illustrator Visit! Part 1 of 4." *KQ Blog*, January 10, 2016; Accessed February 29, 2016. http://knowledgequest.aasl.org/you-too-can-host-an-authorillustrator-visit-1-of-4/.

Wall, Cindy, and Lynn Pawloski. *The Maker Cookbook: Recipes for Children's and 'Tween Library Programs*. Santa Barbara, CA: Libraries Unlimited, 2014.

Young, Terrence E., Jr. "We Celebrate." *School Library Connection* 1, no. 6 (January 2016): 21–23.

CHAPTER 6

Technology

Educators should seek to integrate literacy, rather than integrate technology. If we rethink what it is to be literate in today's information environment, and integrate that, then the technology will come. But it will not come because we are convinced that laying the children's hands on these machines will make them smarter, or better prepared for their future. Computers and the Internet will be an essential part of teaching and learning because they are the tools of contemporary literacy.

—David F. Warlick, *Redefining Literacy 2.0*

Technology continues to grow at an astronomical rate. Everyday there are new applications and tools that students, teachers, and school librarian can use—many of which weren't even invented when the previous edition of this book was published. It can seem daunting to see how they can possibly learn how to use all of these resources or keep up as new ones are coming. Educators need to feel comfortable letting the students show them how to use these technology tools and then, in turn, educators can help students learn more effectively and make good decisions on what to do with the technology.

Many of these technology tools were not originally designed to be tools used in education; however, educators and students are finding ways to make these tools part of the educational landscape. Because many of these tools are open for anyone to use, it is sometimes hard to avoid topics or words that might be inappropriate for young elementary students to see or hear. This does not mean the tools do not have value or should not be used with students but rather one has to be reasonably cautious and more creative in how one can use them with students. Be sure to follow district guidelines and to comply with terms of use of the sites. Talk to students about the potential of finding inappropriate things on the web and what process should they follow if they do.

Technology in Elementary Schools

Throughout the book there have been references to using technology for communication, instruction, and administration of the school library program. Technology is just a part of everyday life, so there is little doubt that it won't be a part of everyday life in an elementary school.

As schools have been embracing technology, the focus continues to be on using it as a tool to help improve learning. Just like a pencil, an overhead projector, and a book have been vehicles to help students learn and create, technology tools, computers, apps, and devices should also be seen as a way to help students learn and grow.

Libraries Leading with Technology

When technology first began entering into schools, many school librarians were early adopters. Often they were in charge of the equipment as well as working to help facilitate people using it. Fast forward many years and technology has grown by leaps and bounds and so has the technology staff needed to keep it functioning. This has not negated the fact that school librarians should still be utilizing technology, being aware of trends, pushing the envelope of possibilities, and helping to ensure students and staff have access to the tools and resources they need. While school librarians might not be in charge of technology, they should be an active voice in promoting it, providing professional development to staff, and in integrating it into the instruction they provide in the school library.

There are many different ways that technology impacts the school library program. In the paragraphs that follow, we'll look at some of them and provide some resources as you explore them.

Automation Systems

Hopefully by now most school libraries are automated. Using the computer to track the ins and outs of resources, providing quick access to materials available in the library, and helping to expand the library beyond the walls with access to eBooks, websites, and more, the automation systems of today provide a valuable function in today's school libraries.

See Figure 6.1 for a list of library automation vendors. Several of the vendors have been in the business for decades and their products have grown and expanded. Many are now web-based for easy access at school and home. Most of them also provide a mobile component for access on multiple devices. Many offer additional features, so when deciding on which system to use, it is important to research the options available. In addition, a lot of systems will offer to host the automation system instead of the district having to set up dedicated servers allowing the vendor to easily update and troubleshoot problems, which can be helpful in some districts.

Alexandria Library Software	www.goalexandria.com
Book Systems	www.booksys.com
Evergreen	evergreen-ils.org
Follett Software Company—Destiny	www.follettlearning.com
Koha	liblime.com
Library World	www.libraryworld.com
Mandarin Library Automation	www.mlasolutions.com
OPALS	www.mediaflex.net
Sirsi/Dynix	www.sirsidynix.com
Surpass	www.surpasssoftware.com
The Library Company	www.tlcdelivers.com

Figure 6.1 Library Automation Vendors.

There are also several vendors for open-source library automation systems. These systems tend to have more options for customizations depending on what you want to pay or what staff you have available to work with the system. Beyond the staff needs, it will be important to know what kind of support is available, and how much work it takes to get the system the way you want. However, they can be less expensive compared to the bigger automation companies.

Databases

See Figure 6.2 for a list of online databases that would be useful for elementary students. Beyond online encyclopedias, the options of various databases have grown drastically in the last several years. The reading levels of materials and the support tool databases have made online information much more accessible to elementary students.

Many of them offer online games, connections to standards, support for professional development, and other resources to help integrate these resources into elementary school library programs. They are very appealing to young students and provide a chance for school librarians to introduce students at a young age to the benefit of databases as a resource.

Collaborative Tools

The list of options of tools available online for students to use for collaboration is huge. From GoogleDrive to wikis to Skype and beyond, it would be impossible to list them all here. Not to mention, the tools seem to come and go or evolve faster than you can write up a description. Instead let's focus on the collaborative nature of these tools and some elements to consider.

First and foremost with any tool, make sure it complies with the district policies and that the site allows elementary student access. Some of the collaborative tools have restrictions for students under the age of 13. It is important that school librarians take the lead in promoting and following the ethical use of these tools.

Consider how the school librarian and classroom teacher want students to work together and then let that drive and determine the tool selected. The instructional goal is the primary focus, and the technology tool is the vehicle to get there. Remember that these tools come and go (or sometimes move from free to fee based), so be ready for Plan B in case something changes. It is good to demonstrate to students that school librarians and teachers can be flexible when necessary.

Let the students help teach how to use these tools. Often they have a better understanding of them than the school librarian and classroom teachers. Let them be the leaders. The role of the school librarian and classroom teachers as facilitators are to focus on how we ethically and appropriately conduct ourselves in using these tools.

These collaborative tools can not only be used to connect our learning spaces beyond the walls of our school but also to other schools in the district, state, country, or world. Consider how to make connections to expand learning beyond the school library or the classroom and how students can learn and interact more with the world around them.

ABDO—abdopublishing.com/our-products/abdo-zoom
ABDO Zoom ✦ *Subscription required*

BrainPop—www.brainpop.com
BrainPop and Brain Pop, Jr.

Britannica—www.britannica.com
Encyclopedia Britannica and ImageQuest

Capstone Publishing—www.capstonepress.com
PebbleGo and PebbleGo Next ✦ *Subscription required*

Credo Reference—corp.credoreference.com
Credo ✦ *Subscription required*

Digital Public Library of America—dp.la
Free

Dorling Kindersely—dkfindout.com/us/
DK Finds Out ✦ *Free*

EBSCOhost—www.ebscohost.com/us-elementary-schools
Variety of database options ✦ *Subscription required*

Gale Cengage—www.cengage.com
Variety of database options ✦ *Subscription required*

International Children's Digital Library Foundation—en.childrenslibrary.org
Free

Lincoln Library Press—www.factcite.com
FactCite ✦ *Subscription required*

One More Story—www.onemorestory.com
Subscription required

ProQuest—www.proquest.com/libraries/schools/
Variety of database options ✦ *Subscription required*

Rosen—www.pklifescience.com
PowerKids Science Databases ✦ *Subscription required*

Scholastic Library—go.grolier.com
Grolier Online ✦ *Subscription required*

TeachingBooks.net—teachingbooks.net
Subscription required

World Book Online—www.worldbookonline.org
Subscription required

Figure 6.2 Online Databases.

Collaboration with these tools can be conversations, written text, file sharing, images and photos, and video. There are all sorts of ways information can be shared with these collaborative tools. There are all kinds of speakers and guests who can be invited into the library (or school) for students to learn from experts in the field. The potential really is amazing for interacting with these collaborative sites.

Finally, it is important to consider that while we have focused on how these collaborative tools can help students learn, also think in terms of how they can make the school librarians' jobs easier, how school librarians can interact with their colleagues around the district, state, and world, and how school librarians can use these tools to collaborate with their staff as well.

Best Websites/Best Apps

Since 2009, the American Association of School Librarians (AASL) has been publishing an annual list of the Best Websites for Teaching and Learning. This list is a great place to gain ideas of the tools (and how to use them with students) that can be very effective in a school environment. People can access all the lists since 2009 at http://www.ala.org/aasl/standards/best/websites. There are resource for supporting and promoting these tools with faculty and staff. In addition, there are some free webinars for some of the tools to give school librarians and other educators ideas for integrating these tools into the classroom.

Following the success of the Best Websites list, in 2013 AASL began awarding an annual list of the Best Apps for Teaching and Learning. Modeled under the same principle, these apps are some of the best tools and resources for use on various devices. Again, AASL also provides extensive support material and resources, http://www.ala.org/aasl/standards/best/apps Past lists are also available.

Every year in June, the new list of Websites and Apps are announced at the American Library Association conference. Following the conference, they are then posted online. When school librarians are looking for a place to start with websites and apps, this is the place to begin.

1:1 Environments

Many schools are moving to a 1:1 environment where each student has his or her own personal device—whether it be iPads, Chromebooks, and so on. Typically, it has started at the high school level and has been working down to the elementary level. There are many considerations for the school librarian to think about as this is rolled out in the school.

Some possible things to think about:

◆ Should the school librarian be part of tracking the devices? Can the automation system help with checking them in/out?

◆ How can the school librarian be part of providing professional development for students and staff?

- How is instruction going to need to be altered?
- How can the school librarian take advantage of the move to 1:1 to increase collaborative opportunities?
- How does the 1:1 environment change the collection development plan?
- How can the school librarian be part of the leadership team making the decisions about the 1:1 roll out, resources and tools, and implementation plans?

1:1 environments greatly alter how things are done in school. It is important because school librarian is out in front ensuring the school library program is providing services and resources, instruction and professional development, and demonstrating how the school library program and school librarians are even more important and relevant in the 1:1 environment than they were ever before.

1:1 environments do not replace the school library or school librarian just like videos or eBooks have not replaced the printed book. Instead, it means that services and instruction have to alter to include the new tools and formats they bring. The proactive school librarian must demonstrate their relevance and how the school library program is even more important with a 1:1 environment.

Social Networks

In Chapter 3, we talked about how the school library can use social networks as a way to communicate with parents, staff, administrators, and the community. These communications can be most helpful in building advocates about what the school library program does and the value it has for students and staff.

The topic keeps coming back up anytime you think about technology today. It is important that school librarians stay current with the trends and uses that information to help educate their teachers, administrators, and parents. It is also important to have conversations with students about the appropriate ways to interact with these tools. The school librarian should be a leader in digital citizenship instruction.

Learning Management Systems (LMS)

As districts move to 1:1 environment, they are looking for systems to help organize students, teachers, curriculum, and courses. Learning management systems (LMS such as Canvas or Black-Board) provide the function for assignments, discussions, sharing content, video, audio, and keeping track of grades all in one spot. School librarians have to make sure to create a library presence in these virtual environments whether it be a class that all students and staff are subscribed to, or links that are accessible from any course, to access for discussions and help when needed.

If an LMS hasn't started in the district, make sure the library is part of the conversations from the beginning. If there is already an LMS, make sure the library is integrated into it. There are many options and opportunities, and it is important that the school library is there.

Technology Policies and Procedures

Technology polices are usually adopted by the school board based on recommendations from the superintendent and/or director of technology. The overarching document is the Acceptable Use Policy that students and staff sign. These documents provide guidance on what is and what is not permitted in the district. Beyond that, there could be a variety of other documents that provide procedures or policies dictating how staff and students will use technology.

First and foremost, it is important the school librarian be well versed in all these documents. Knowledge will help when collaborating with teachers and deciding on potential projects and technology tools to use with those projects. In addition, make sure to know the process and procedures in asking for changes to the policies. Technology continues to grow and change rapidly. Policies written just a year ago could now be out of date and stifle student learning. School librarians who hit roadblocks will want to draft a document that demonstrates why the policy should be changed and how it impacts students and student learning. The administration might not agree to alter the policies. However, it could avoid creating a situation where there is animosity between technology department and the school librarian, or administration and the school librarian.

Filters

As part of national legislation, schools have installed filters on all machines in the building. The tools are designed to protect students from the inappropriate content on the web. Filters are not 100 percent foolproof, and often in attempting to block inappropriate content, valuable and useful resources and information are also blocked.

This is the opportunity for the school librarian to be seen as a leader in the building. How can the school librarian build a bridge between the content and teachers need or want and the guidelines and rules the technology department has to follow? There needs to be a clearly defined process and timeline for asking for websites to be unblocked. The school librarian could be part of opening the door in creating that process.

Another opportunity is to investigate options that might be easier for all involved. For example, one district has filter software installed, but all staff has a login/password to override the filter for work-related searches. While it is tracked every time they override the filter, it does give staff the ability to check out a website before asking for it to be unblocked or the ability to get the information the student needs in a timely manner.

Copyright/Creative Commons

It is hard to determine where to place some topics because they permeate throughout the school library program. Copyright is one of them and is a huge part of the instructional and professional development role of the school librarian. While school librarians are not lawyers, they can still help guide teachers and students on ethical and legal uses of both print and online resources. They should be leading in helping to research what is permissible and what is not permissible. The copyright laws are massive, but many resources for school librarians by authors like Carol Simpson are great guides. If it isn't clear, ask to have the district consult with the district attorney for a final verdict.

Beyond copyright, Creative Commons licensing is an important element for school librarians to understand. Copyright holders can expand the options or rights they give to others by using a Creative Commons license. Therefore, if someone creates a photo, they can give permission from the beginning for user to alter it or use it in commercial works, https://creativecommons.org/about/.

Work Cited

Warlick, David F. *Redefining Literacy 2.0*, 2nd edition. Columbus, OH: Linworth Publishing, 2009.

Further Reading

Bell, Mary Ann, Holly Weimar, and James L. van Roekel. *School Librarians and the Technology Department: A Practical Guide to Successful Collaboration*. Santa Barbara, CA: Linworth Publishing, 2013.

Berger, Pam, and Sally Trexler. *Choosing Web 2.0 Tools for Learning and Teaching in a Digital World*. Santa Barbara, CA: Libraries Unlimited, 2010.

Johnson, Doug. *The Classroom Teacher's Technology Survival Guide*. Charlottesville, VA: Wiley, John & Sons, 2012.

Simpson, Carol A. *Copyright for Administrators*. Worthington, OH: Linworth Publishing, 2008.

Simpson, Carol A. *Copyright for Schools: A Practical Guide*, 5th edition. Santa Barbara, CA: Linworth Publishing, 2010.

Simpson, Carol A. "Copyright Question of the Month." *School Library Connection* 30, no. 2 (October 2011): 22.

Zmuda, Allison, and Violet H. Harada. *Librarians as Learning Specialists: Meeting the Learning Imperative for the 21st Century*. Westport, CT: Libraries Unlimited, 2008.

CHAPTER 7

How is what I'm going to do today going to impact student achievement?

— Carl A. Harvey II

It is the author's opinion that every school librarian should ask that question every day! There are always administrative things to do to run the library, but student achievement is the school librarian's primary goal because that is the school's primary goal. This chapter focuses on the administrative role of the school librarian and how to make that easier in order to focus on the primary role of impacting student achievement.

Policies and Procedures

Throughout this book there have been many references to knowing and complying with the districts policies and procedures. It is critical as a school librarian to know what the policies and procedures are and where to find them whenever there is a question.

Policies are the guiding documents from the school board or administration on how the school library should be run. Policies might include a technology policy, selection policy, challenged materials policy, collection development policy, or even the type of schedule a library operates. School librarians often provide inputs or suggestions as policies are created, while the final decision rests with an administrator and/or the school board.

Procedures are step-by-step instructions on how to complete a specific task. Procedures could be for students, teachers, library staff, or the school librarian. Procedures provide a blueprint so that there is no confusion about how to complete a certain task. Procedures are typically developed by the school librarian and do not require approval by the school board. Make sure to share them with the principal so that he or she can be on the same wavelength. The administrator will let the school librarian know if he or she has concerns. This is a great opportunity for discussion about all the "behind-the-scenes" things that a school librarian does that often no one realizes is happening.

Procedures are part of creating an environment that is safe for students and a place where they feel comfortable. School librarians know from the very beginning the expectations and the process for completing the most common tasks in the space. It is a great way for behavior management in a school library because there is no doubt that from the first day they walk in the door until the day they leave—that is what is expected of them.

It is a good idea to include stakeholders in creating the procedures. It may be difficult to write procedures with every class in the school with hundreds of students. The school library needs to have consistent procedures for all grades, so consider using the student library advisory group to write the procedures. When students are part of the development process, they have more ownership of the procedures. The process is the same for procedures for other groups. For example, consider asking the library advisory committee to help write any procedures for the staff.

When policies and procedures are clearly written and shared with stakeholders, there is a common understanding on how the school library is to run. It eliminates confusion and allows the program to run smoothly. Some possible areas or ideas for procedures could include circulation, ordering, processing materials, daily "to-do" items, weekly "to-do" items, monthly "to-do" items, beginning of the year checklist, end of the year checklist, student behavior and expectations, and recess procedures. Policies and procedures are necessary to ensure that everyone can take full advantage of everything the school library has to offer.

School Library Policies

Policies might (or should) include a selection of instructional materials policy, a challenge policy, and an acceptable use of policy for technology. If these policies don't exist, initiate the conversation to begin developing them. Follow the proper chain of command in talking with the building administrator and central office administrators who might coordinate the school library program and then the superintendent. Make sure to have examples and data to support the needed policies.

Some districts set very specific policies such as check out limits or flexible versus fixed schedules for the entire district, whereas other districts will allow the individual buildings to make those decisions.

School librarians in the 21st century will want to keep up with how the landscape is changing in their school libraries. What policies will need to be created to deal with new formats and resources in the collection? What policies will need to be created (or modified) to bring in the new technology tools available to students and staff?

Collection Development Guidelines from Montana

http://msl.mt.gov/slr/cmpolsch.html

Resources for the School Librarian

http://www.sldirectory.com/libsf/resf/coldev2.html

School Library Policies from California

http://www.cde.ca.gov/ci/cr/lb/policies.asp

Workbook for Selection Policy Writing

http://www.ala.org/bbooks/challengedmaterials/preparation/workbook-selection-policy-writing

Figure 7.1 Sample Policies.

Throughout the book, issues about ethical concerns and intellectual freedom have been raised. It can be important when reviewing policies that the school librarian has conversations with administrators about these important issues. How do school librarians protect student privacy? How do school librarians make student sure that students have access to the information they need? How do school librarians make sure items aren't banned from the collection? This would be a great time to review the *ALA Intellectual Freedom Manual* and see how the district policies match with the philosophy of the field.

It is quite possible that the district policies and/or procedures may be out of line with the theory and practice in the field. School librarians have to be political in their work with administrators when it comes to policy revision and reform. Look for opportunities for discussion. Consider the change for when a policy change or revision might be possible. Come armed with data and facts. Remember that it may be a gradual change rather than everything the school librarian wants. Also consider that sometimes those in charge may not be open to change. (See Figure 7.1 for some sample policy links.)

School Library Procedures
Student Procedures

Student procedures could include things like: how to check out a book, how to use a shelf marker, or how to select a book. (See Figure 7.2 for sample procedures). Procedures should be positive and detailed. These procedures give students clear expectations for completing a task. When there are problems or behavior issues, referring to the procedures while discussing the issue with students provides a clear picture of what the students were supposed to be doing. Creating common procedures throughout the building also produce a consistent environment for students. They know the expectation no matter where in the school they go.

Procedures drastically cut down on discipline issues. Not following procedures should have a natural consequence. It could be the elimination of something fun to give time to practice the procedures that were not being followed.

Consider taking video of students who are following correct procedures. Use these on the morning announcements or as part of a lesson to review the procedure with other students. Post them on the school website so that parents can see the expectation of students doing the right thing.

Procedures should be posted. Tape checkout procedures to the checkout desk. Hang up procedures for the Story Steps area of the library in the Story Steps area. In elementary schools, this not only reinforces the procedures but also is another place where students will find text to read. Procedures can also be posted online, kept in binders, or are written on a poster to hang on the wall. Whatever the format, the important thing is that they are easily accessible and visible.

Chime Procedures

When you hear the chimes, use **COOPERATION** to stop what you are doing and listen for directions.

Story Steps Procedures

Use **EFFORT** to come into the Story Steps quietly.

Use **COMMON SENSE** to walk up and down the Story Steps.

Use **RESPONSIBILITY** to keep your hands and feet to yourself.

Use **INTEGRITY** to be an active listener.

iPad Procedures

Use **RESPECT** to check out an iPad.

Students will need to use **ORGANIZATION** to keep track of the iPad.

Use **CURIOSITY** and **CREATIVITY** to use the iPad for schoolwork and projects.

Use **EFFORT** to make sure to handle the iPad with care.

Use **COOPERATION** to share the iPad with other students in the classroom.

Use **COMMON SENSE** to charge the iPad so it can be used by others when needed.

Recess Procedures

• Students are welcome to come to the library media center during recess.
• Students will:
   – use **RESPECT** to not disturb classes who are using the library media center.
   – use **RESPONSIBILITY** to ask for permission to leave the library during recess.
   –use **CURIOSITY** to quietly play with the puppets, read a book, read a magazine, explore the math or writing center, and/or find a quiet place to spend recess.
   – use **COMMON SENSE** when playing with the puppets to choose one puppet at a time and returning puppets back to the puppet stands.
   – use **INTEGRITY** to watch the clock and return back to class when recess is over.

Book Check Out Procedures

Use **COMMON SENSE** to check out the number of items for which you can be responsible.

Fiction books check out for two weeks; all other items check out for one week.

You may renew an item one time unless another student is waiting for the item.

Use **RESPONSIBILITY** to return your books on time. Overdue items must be returned to check out new items.

Use **PATIENCE** to ask to put a book on reserve, if it is currently checked out.

Use **RESPONSIBILITY** to find a nice and safe place to keep library materials while they are at home. If materials are lost or damaged, students will have to pay the replacement cost.

Figure 7.2 Sample Student Procedures.

Staff Procedures/Processes

Procedures for staff are also a smart idea. It creates a common understanding and can help foster a collegial working environment. Some examples might include procedures for signing up or scheduling time to work with the school librarian, bringing their classes to the school library, textbook distribution, accessing technology resources, or laminating resources. See Figure 7.3 for sample staff procedures.

Library Staff Procedures/Processes

Procedures for library support staff are going to cover many of the day-to-day operations. They could also include procedures for volunteers, student helpers, and so forth. Procedures also help library support staff because it relieves the burden of being the decision maker when working with students and teachers. They are merely following the procedures that were already outlined. Procedures give them clear guidance when a decision needs to be made. Procedures should be written down and kept together for easy access. Procedures in turn also become a training manual when staff or volunteers move on. See Figure 7.4 for sample library staff procedures.

As part of those procedures, there could be systems in place for keeping track of what needs to be done. One librarian used a dry erase board, and the librarian and support staff kept track of "to-do" items. Another used a Google Doc and/or Google Calendars to help keep in step on what projects needed to be done and the priority it had.

School Librarian Procedures/Processes

In order to make the job of the school librarian easier, if there are repetitive tasks that the school librarian performs, it could be useful to write them down. They can be helpful reminders year after year. For example, maybe procedures list steps that the librarian must do in the beginning and at the end of the school year. A list of procedures for budgets and ordering would be helpful. These guides can be helpful when memories fail (and that happens to the best of us) and can be helpful when a librarian retires or moves on to the next adventure; it can be a good guide for the next librarian to consider.

Writing it all out can create a powerful advocacy tool. It can demonstrate all the steps involved, the estimated time involved, and can really show someone what it takes to run a library. At the same time, it can also give chance for some reflection. Are there some things in the procedures that can go and save more time for instruction and working with students and staff?

Facilities

The school library space is sometimes one of the biggest spaces in the school. The space houses the collection, provides space for instruction and students to work, gives the librarian

Poster Maker Machine Procedures

+ Posters made on the Poster Maker cost the school approximately $4.00 per poster. Please make sure the settings are correct before you start printing. We don't want to waste paper by having to reprint mistakes.
+ Place items face down.
+ Press Start/Clear

Please see a library assistant if you need assistance.

Laminating Procedures

+ Please make sure to choose items that will have lasting value to laminate.
+ Items will be laminated on Monday and Wednesday.
+ Items dropped off by 10am, should be ready by the end of the day.
+ Items will be put in teacher's mailboxes for pick-up.

Whom Do I Ask?	
School Librarian	Collaboration for instruction, instructional materials (print, nonprint, and computer), leveled library, interlibrary loan requests, reading incentive program, WNOR Studios, LMC Webpage resources, and professional development
Tech or Library Assistant	Problems with voice mail, e-mail, computer networking, computer problems, printer problems, printer cartridges, simple software assistance questions, and overhead bulbs
Tech or Library Assistant	Circulation problems, lost books, and overdue books
School Librarian	Technology hardware, software, and A/V needs (ordering additional copies of software, replacing old equipment, etc.) school librarian will work with the principal
School Librarian	Anything else? We're sure there are things we've missed. So, if there is, let me know and we'll figure out who can best help.

Figure 7.3 Sample Staff Procedures.

Opening Procedures

Turn on all computers.

Unlock and open all doors.

Check voicemail and email.

Login / Setup automation system.

Check in any materials in the book drop.

Check calendar for today's schedule and special events.

Freshen up any displays with new titles.

Check "To Do List" dry erase board.

Weekly Procedures

Water the plants

Back-up the Automation System

Run Overdue Notices

Run Reserve Pick-up Notices

Check to see what needs to be done to keep the library neat and organized.

Processing Materials Procedures

The librarian will have cataloged the book.

Print spine labels and barcode from the automation system.

Attach spine labels and barcodes in the appropriate places.
(spine label 1" from the bottom on the spine and the barcode on the upper left corner of back of the book)

Cover the book with the appropriate material.
(Mylar jackets for book jackets / paperbacks with paperback protectors)

Change the book from "on order" to "available" in the catalog.

Put the book out for students to enjoy.

Figure 7.4 Sample Library Staff Procedures.

some working space, and can often be the hub for many other special events. A well-designed school library can have multiple events and activity happening at the same time.

School librarians often think of facilities when they talk about access, so it is important to consider the users. How do the special education people have access to the resources? How do students who are color-blind utilize the library if they use colorful signs or stickers on books? Are there appropriate areas for someone in a wheelchair? Are there ways for all students to utilize the library's services and facilities?

Use

First and foremost, the schedule of the library and the size of the library dictate how the space can be utilized. If the library operates on a fixed schedule, the librarian obviously needs some sort of dedicated space for instruction. However, if the library has a table/chairs area and a story area, a schedule could be set up to allow others to use the space the librarian isn't using for instruction. This would work in a flexible environment, too. One librarian had several distinct spaces—two instructional areas, a computer lab, story steps area, and then the area where the collection is housed for circulation. The librarian didn't keep a schedule for circulation but did have a schedule for each of the spaces. As she worked with classes, she reserved the space she needed but allowed the other spaces to be utilized by the rest of the school. Therefore, teachers were able to reserve the story steps for guest speakers, or one of the table/chairs areas for a special project. It allowed the space to be utilized for as many different things as possible.

Depending on staffing, the library can be utilized far beyond plans for instruction. Small groups and individuals could come down to work, to research, to explore during recess, and to use the makerspaces. There are so many ways the space can be used. Each library and spaces is different, but thinking in terms of how to maximize the use is important.

When designing new schools, some architects and administrators are wondering why someone might still need a school library space. It isn't just about housing a collection of books and materials, but rather the activity and work that happens there. Showing how to maximize the space can help them to see why the school library space is so important.

One alarming trend is the use of the school library facility as a testing center. One librarian counted that she lost 60+ days in her library to testing. Obviously, school librarians have no control of testing mandates and often no control of the schedule, but it is important to document the time the facility is unavailable to students. If the facility is lost to testing, how do services continue? Can the school librarian teach in the classroom? Can he or she bring a book cart throughout the school, so books can still circulate? It is not ideal, but the services and instruction students need are critical, so looking for options for maintaining that should be the first priority. Collecting data to demonstrate what is lost when the library is closed may be necessary to help change opinions and minds about the effective use of the space.

Layout

The layout of the library also makes a difference. One librarian had an instructional space in the middle with the bookshelves around it. It was far more difficult for classes to be checking out while the librarian was teaching. Another librarian had a dedicated space for instruction away from the collection that allowed multiple events to be happening at the same time.

Sometimes school librarians can control the space, but other times they are stuck with whatever space is given. The point is to think outside the box about how to make it work. One librarian got shelves, tables, and chairs that were all movable allowing for reconfiguration of the space when authors would visit or if there were several classes in the library at the same time.

Often a library makeover makes a great grant request from a PTO or other sources. Design what kind of facility the students need. Research the trends. See what other librarians are doing and then see what might be possible. One never knows what might happen if they never ask.

Design/Decorations/Displays

Colors, decorations, and design are all about attracting people to the library.

The library has to be vibrant and full of life. Plants, lighting, fun spaces for reading and exploring, Makerspaces, LEGO walls, puppets, and all sorts of other things can be huge attractions for students to want to come to the library to learn and explore. Consider how the library appeals to students.

Sometimes color can do wonders to brighten up a library. If the school librarian has a dated and drab library facility, talk with the administrator about being able to paint it to freshen it up. Think about the decorations on the wall. Do they have a point? Beyond the library procedures, which should be posted, are they just a bunch of posters, or do the decorations help with the library's instructional mission.

One librarian's mother loved to make quilts, so he had them hanging all over the library. He had several LEGO sets he had put together as a child, so he brought those in to decorate the shelves. Every time he went on a trip overseas, he would bring back something to add to the library décor.

Displays are a great way to introduce students to new resources, reintroduce them to old resources, guide them to certain parts of the library, or to highlight or promote events and instruction happening in the library. Consider letting teachers know that they can set up a "museum" type exhibit of student work. The art teacher might like to have a display of student projects. Use the facility to show off the final projects that include time in the library (and make that library connection obvious to the viewer).

Students will always gravitate toward certain materials. Typically, those aren't the things to display. Instead reintroduce them to a new series of book. Display books by new authors. Highlight materials that might vanish just on the shelf. It is amazing the increase in circulation that will come from a display of books.

In the elementary library, consider what elements to display on top of the shelves. Whether it is books, plants, stuffed animals, or other objects. Especially at elementary, there is a great opportunity to maximize the librarian's time. Put a stuffed animal of a dog and cat next to the pet books. Put stuffed animals or signs of favorite characters throughout the Everyone/Enjoyable/Picture Book section. Leave the globe near the country and state books. While choosing books to display, pick from books that the students might find in that area. It will help them to find more if they like the first one.

One of the displays on the wall should also be the library's procedures for easy reference for students. Include procedures near any area of materials that might be different. One library had procedures that hung above the puppets that were taped to the wall near the LEGO table and posted in the story steps. The procedures need to be near where the action is.

Library conference and events are great places to get posters and other fun types of things to make the walls colorful and attractive to students. Helping to create the look of the library could also be part of a makerspace activity or the library advisory committee to offer suggestions.

The atmosphere of the school library is so important. Students should feel welcomed and want to come to the library. Displays can help create that environment for students and staff.

Schedules

Fixed or flexible schedule? While primarily an elementary school library issue, the type of schedule a school library operates on has long been debated in the field. (See Figure 7.5 for a comparison of how the different types of schedules impact collection, instruction, and facilities.) Often it is out of the control of most school librarians as the schedule is dictated by administration. Most would agree that flexible is the ideal but the reality in many elementary schools across the country is that the school library program is on a fixed schedule. In the November 2001 *School Library Journal*, Doug Johnson wrote one of the most infamous articles in the flexible versus fixed debate "It's Good to Be Inflexible," www.doug-johnson.com/dougwri/real-flexibility.html, in which he gave his rationale for fixed schedules. On his website, readers can also see the pro and con responses he received (Figure 7.5).

Fixed schedules give every student a regular scheduled opportunity to be in the school library. The school librarian provides preparation time for teachers, so the teacher usually does not remain with the students. School librarians are responsible for instruction and also for the time that students check out materials.

Flexible scheduling of the school library provides no formal schedule. Students come to check out materials whenever they want. Instruction relies on the school librarian collaborating with

ACCESS TO THE COLLECTION

Fixed: With this model, classes go to the library on a set schedule once a week to check out materials. The only time they can check out materials is during this slot. Typically, the classroom teacher is not present during checkout. Also, this time is often connected with library instruction. The fixed model is most heavily used to provide teacher planning time during the school day. The library is scheduled much like other specials areas of art, music, and physical education. This schedule guarantees that every student is checking out every week (or every few days). However, students often can't come throughout the week, even if they run out of materials.

Flexible: With this model, classes (or students) go to the library to check out new materials whenever they want. They can actually go to the library multiple times in the same day, if needed. Typically, the classroom teacher is present during checkout and is often out mingling among the students helping them to locate materials. The flexible model separates circulation from library instruction. One advantage is that it is very easy to adjust the schedule based on such events as holidays, assemblies, and specials events. The teacher is also present to help guide students based on their needs. While that is also a pro, it can be a con if teachers are limiting what students can check out. If the librarian is teaching or helping other students, the teacher can be an added set of hands to help circulation run smoothly (operating the automation system, helping students, etc.).

Hybrid: With this model, there are all kinds of options. One possibility would be that students have a fixed time each week to go to the library and check out books as a class. But, there can also be open times in the schedule where students can check out if they need additional resources before their next scheduled visit. The pro is that this approach offers a consistent time but at the same time gives access if students need additional resources. The con is that students cannot access the library resources if that additional time doesn't fit with the teacher's schedule.

OTHER THINGS TO CONSIDER:
  + While very few libraries are totally digital, how do eBooks fit into the equation for determining schedules?
  + Is having the teacher in the library a pro or a con for students checking out materials?
  + What kinds of expectations are established for circulation on a flexible schedule (i.e., do all students have an opportunity to check out once a week)?
  + Is it possible to set up a self-checkout option to free up staff from being "chained" to the circulation desk?

INSTRUCTION

Perhaps the most important role of the school librarian is working with students. How might that best be scheduled?

Fixed: With this model, the librarian is providing instruction to students while teachers have their planning time, so the teacher is usually not present. In this model, since circulation is also part of that block of time, the amount of instruction time can vary. Rotations vary but often this means instruction happens every four to six days. Collaboration can work in this model with the librarian connecting instruction to what is happening in the classroom but the rotation and lack of the teacher not present makes it more difficult.

Flexible: With this model, the librarian is providing instruction at the point of need for students. The teacher and the librarian have co-planned, will co-teach, and often co-assess the work of students. Students often will come for multiple visits in consecutive days for instruction and to work on an assigned project. This allows for a class to focus on a project and complete it in a timely manner. Depending on space and staffing, the librarian can juggle between multiple classes scheduled in the library or provide instruction in the classroom as well. The librarian is much more available to accommodate classes on an as-needed basis.

Hybrid: With this model, the students go to the library for a fixed time each week for instruction, but the librarian can also provide instruction at the point of need. This can be accomplished by having "open times" in the schedule when a fixed class is not scheduled, or perhaps by having an assistant cover the fixed time while the librarian is free to provide instruction at the point of need. (The librarian prepares materials that the assistant uses to cover the fixed time.) The fixed class does not have the teacher present, but during the "open times" for point-of-need instruction, the teacher is present and actively participating.

Figure 7.5   Flex/Fixed/Hybrid Chart for Schedules

OTHER THINGS TO CONSIDER:
- ✦ Does instruction and circulation have to be connected?
- ✦ How can it be ensured that instruction in the library connects to what is happening in the classroom?
- ✦ If the teacher is not part of the planning, delivering, and assessing, how can communication be maintained between the librarian and the classroom teacher?
- ✦ How can it be ensured that all students have the opportunity to work with the librarian?
- ✦ How is the librarian part of planning and curriculum design if he or she is working with fixed classes all day?

FACILITIES

School librarians operate one of the largest spaces in the school. It is, therefore, natural that there may be opportunities to utilize the facility beyond instruction and circulation.

Fixed: With this model, the librarian is responsible for the library. Because they are responsible for the children they are instructing, they are unable to supervise independent users or other groups. The library is the librarian's classroom, so they are utilizing the space available. Likely there is not room or the option for other groups to utilize the space.

Flexible: With this model, the librarian is free to provide instruction and work with students anywhere, so it is possible that he or she is in the classrooms or other spaces, which means the library story area or instructional area could be available for others to use. For example, a Google Calendar could be used for each space. The librarian would reserve the space when he or she is using it for instruction, but otherwise it would be available for others. Guest speakers, classes needing tables to spread out materials, or just a different place to work could all utilize the library space. Other educators who want to work with small groups could also utilize space in the library if it is not being used.

Hybrid: Likely, the library is full in this model, but there could be opportunities for the facility to be used by others in the school day, too. It really will vary greatly depending on just what type of hybrid scheduling is being utilized.

OTHER THINGS TO CONSIDER:
- ✦ What is the size of the library? Are there opportunities for multiple things to be happening at once?
- ✦ What "spaces" are there? For example, is there a story area, instructional areas, conference rooms? How can that space be best utilized?
- ✦ How is scheduling handled for the spaces that are available for others to use? Would a Google Calendar work?
- ✦ Should the library facility have other uses?

Source: Harvey, Carl A., II. "The Schedule Spectrum." School Library Monthly 31, no. 3 (December 2014): 17–19.

Figure 7.5   Continued

the classroom teacher. Students from a particular class or grade level may come down for several days in a row to work on a unit and then it may be a few weeks before they are back for the next project. This flexibility allows the school librarian to work in depth with students rather than just once every few days for a set amount of time.

Either schedule relies heavily on the building administrator and on the school librarian. The administrator has the control over how the schedule is organized in the building unless the schedule is based on a contract with the teacher's union. If it is not a state or district mandate, the administrator can determine if the library will operate on a fixed or flexible schedule. The administrator can also be a driving factor when a flexible schedule is implemented. If the administrator expects teachers to work with the school librarian, then he or she can make sure that all students have the instruction and opportunities in the school library. The same kind of impact can be felt based on the role the school librarian takes. On a fixed schedule, while it can be more difficult due to time constraints, the school librarian can still work to collaborate with teachers and connect instruction in the school library to what is being taught in the classroom. On the flexible schedule side, the school librarian needs to be the proactive element who goes out to work with teachers. He or she needs to be touting the skills students need to learn and suggesting opportunities where the classroom teacher and school librarian can work together to design instruction.

Peggy Milam Creighton in her November 2007 article in *Library Media Connection* "Just How Flexible Are We?" updates the status of implementing flexible scheduling. She summarizes the current research that says more than half of the elementary schools in the country are on a fixed schedule and the majority are either fixed or a combination despite the research saying flexible schedules are more beneficial for student achievement.

Looking at the 21st-century students and the skills they will need, it becomes harder and harder to squeeze those into 40 minute lessons every few days. Students (and teachers) will need to devote more time for students to work on projects. They'll need support from the school librarian at different points along the way. The fixed schedule will make that difficult for students to get access to the school library and school librarian at the point of need.

Beyond just instruction and circulation, the facility itself becomes limited on a fixed schedule. Many media centers not only have an instructional area of tables and chairs but also a story step area as well as an area with all the shelving. Sometimes these are separate areas and sometimes they are intertwined. When the areas are separated the facility can be utilized by more than one class. A flexible schedule school library could accommodate many classes at the same time all doing different things. For example, class A could be at the table and chairs area working on a research project, class B could be in the story area performing a readers theater or listening to a guest speaker, classes C and D could be checking out books, and class E might also be doing research in a computer lab adjacent to the school library. This does not include individual students who might be using the school library for a variety of activities including research, recreational reading, and so forth. The largest classroom in the schools becomes better utilized when a flexible schedule is implemented.

The *Empowering Learners: Guidelines for School Library Programs*, published by AASL in 2009, lists flexible scheduling as the ideal for all school libraries. Everyone knows that often the schedule is out of the hands of the school librarian. However, it is important to be aware of the best practice, aware of the needs of the students, and be able to articulate those to people who can make those decisions because that's what children of the 21st century are going to need.

Calendar Options

If the school librarian is on a flexible or hybrid schedule, consider scheduling tools to help maximize the time for collaboration. Use and share a Google Calendar with the staff. Google Calendar makes it easy to track when the school librarian is available and when they are already booked. The calendars could also be used to track space (as mentioned earlier) or things like mobile carts and other technology tools.

Administering the school library is often the part of the program that goes completely unnoticed. However, school librarians know it is a big part of the job of creating an effective school library program for students. While the primary focus should be on student achievement and working with students and staff, the administrative side of the job of school librarian cannot be ignored either.

Works Cited

American Association of School Librarians. *Empowering Learners: Guidelines for School Library Programs.* Chicago, IL: American Association of School Librarians, 2007.

American Association of School Librarians. *Standards for the 21st Century Learner.* Chicago, IL: American Association of School Librarians, 2007.

Creighton, Peggy Milam. "Just How Flexible Are We?" *Library Media Connection* 26, no. 3 (November 2007): 10, 12–14.

Harvey, Carl A., II. "The Schedule Spectrum." *School Library Monthly* 31, no. 3 (December 2014): 17–19.

Johnson, Doug. "It's Good to Be Inflexible." *School Library Journal* 47, no. 11 (November 2001): 39.

Further Reading

Baule, Steven M. *Facilities Planning for School Library and Technology Centers*, 2nd edition. Santa Barbara, CA: Linworth Publishing, 2007.

Butler, Rebecca P. *School Libraries 3.0: Principles and Practices for the Digital Age.* Lanham, MD: Rowman & Littlefield Education, 2015.

Donham, Jean. *Enhancing Teaching and Learning: A Leadership Guide for School Librarians*, 3rd edition. Chicago, IL: Neal-Schuman, an imprint of the American Library Association, 2014.

Donnelly, Andria C. *The Library Collaboration and Flexible Scheduling Toolkit*. Santa Barbara, CA: Libraries Unlimited, 2015.

Harland, Pamela Colburn. *The Learning Commons: Seven Simple Steps to Transform Your Library*. Santa Barbara, CA: Libraries Unlimited, 2011.

Johnson, Doug. *The Indispensable Librarian: Surviving and Thriving in School Libraries in the Information Age*, 2nd edition. Columbus, OH: Linworth Publishing, 2013.

Magi, Trina, and Martin Garnar, eds. *Intellectual Freedom Manual*. Chicago: ALA Editions, 2015.

Martimo, Susan, and Santa Clara County Office of Education. *Where Do I Start? A School Library Handbook*, 2nd edition. Santa Barbara, CA: Linworth Publishing, 2012.

Repman, Judi, and Gail K. Dickinson, eds. *School Library Management*. Santa Barbara, CA: Linworth Publishing, 2014.

Sullivan, Margaret. *Library Spaces for 21st-Century Learners: A Planning Guide for Creating New School Library Concepts*. Chicago, IL: Association for Library Collections & Technical Services, 2013.

Woolls, Blanche, Ann C. Weeks, and Sharon Coatney. *The School Library Manager*. Santa Barbara, CA: Libraries Unlimited, 2013.

CHAPTER 8

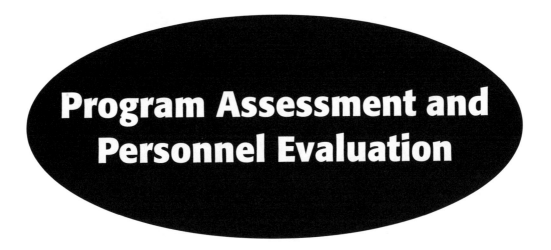

Program Assessment and
Personnel Evaluation

The way in which the library program benefits from evaluation is directly related to how effective the librarian is in addressing each concern.

— Ann M. Martin, *Seven Steps to an Award-Winning School Library Program*

Everyone needs to take time to go back and reflect on where they are and where they want to go. Assessment and evaluations provide us with the data to begin that process of moving forward. The forward thinking school librarian is always looking for ways to improve the program, so the assessment takes stock of where the program is currently. The assessment then can provide the starting point on where to go next. Is the library on track to reach the vision? Does the school librarian need to alter the course or find a new path? What kinds of changes (if any) are going to keep the library program moving forward?

Evaluating the School Library Program

It is important to undertake the process of evaluating the school library program. Decisions made in today's schools are data driven. An important role for school librarians is to collect data for the programs. They need to see what is working and what needs improvement. One way to get better is to analyze the data and determine strategies to implement. School librarians need to know if they are providing the services, the resources, and the opportunities that students and teachers need and want.

Collecting Data
Surveys

The simplest way to find out what people think is to ask. A quick survey is easy to send out and get responses back. Traditional paper and pencil surveys can easily go into mailboxes, but consider using one of the online survey tools such as SurveyMonkey, Zoomerrang, or Polldaddy. Online survey tools can instantly calculate and provide the results of the survey. See Figure 8.1 for a sample annual staff survey and Figure 8.2 for an annual student survey. By just tweaking the survey from year to year, the school librarian can see trends and determine potential areas for improvement or change.

Anecdotal Conversations

Listen to what students, staff, administrators, and parents say about the school library program. Take all their suggestions as constructive. Consider how what they say about the program can be used to make it better. What advice warrants changes in the program? What advice is best to ignore? The school librarian will have to filter out some mean comments because the people saying them often don't have the context for what they are saying. If people are connecting to the messages of what you are trying to accomplish and are saying things that aren't on target, it would lead one to wonder why? Is there something the librarian can do to change their minds?

Other pieces of anecdotal data are the e-mails, notes, and cards that the school librarian receives from students, staff, and parents. Consider creating a "happy" file. This is a place to file letters, notes, or cards. As e-mails have become more of a method for communication, create a file on the computer to download those e-mails that contain praise for the program and the school librarian. These pieces of data are helpful when telling the story of the school library. At the same time, when things are not going well, take a few minutes to revisit the "happy" file. It will help rejuvenate the school librarian to get up and begin to tackle the problems one might be facing at that point.

Statistics

Libraries offer many opportunities to collect statistics. How many items have been circulated this month? How many classes came in to the school library this month? Statistics are important because they help tell part of the story of what is happening in the school library.

The time and effort required in collecting and analyzing statistics is very important, but do not let it become overwhelmingly time consuming. Just because there are statistics that can be collected, it does not mean all data collection is worthy of collection. The school librarian needs to determine which statistics are really going to tell a compelling and impactful story about the school library program.

Consider a principal whose focus is totally on literacy. The data provided to him or her might show how much the students in his or her building are checking out materials. The per pupil

_____ **Teacher**   _____ **Support Staff**   _____ **Other**

Scale: 1–4 with 1 being the lowest and 4 being the highest. If the question does not apply to your role in the building, just leave it blank.

Instruction	1	2	3	4
1. The school librarian is easily available for co-planning, co-teaching, and co-assessment.				
2. I have co-planned with the school librarian this year.				
3. The school librarian is proactive to suggest ideas for activities or lessons.				
4. I am comfortable going and asking the school librarian for help.				
5. Students are free to come and use the library at any time.				
6. The school librarian regularly communicates with the staff about programming and resources using a variety of methods.				
7. The school librarian provides help to me on an individual basis.				
8. The school librarian provides staff development opportunities.				
9. The school librarian is an integral part of the curriculum instruction at our school.				
10. The school library provides support for reading motivation.				
11. The annual author visit is a good use of time and resources.				
12. The school librarian supports my work in meeting school improvement goals.				
13. The school librarian provides instruction that support school improvement goals.				

14. What are (if any) the stumbling blocks in using the school librarian more to help with instruction of your students?

15. How could the school librarian more effectively help you with instruction?

16. How could the school library program support the school improvement goals?

Figure 8.1   Sample Staff Survey.

Facilities and Resources

		1	2	3	4
17.	The school library facility is welcoming and inviting.				
18.	The school library is always available when I need it.				
19.	My students come at least once a week to check out new materials.				
20.	I use the school library catalog in my classroom.				
21.	I use the library catalog with state standards search.				
22.	I use video streaming resources				
23.	I use electronic databases available from the library.				
24.	The school library has sufficient resources to meet the curriculum.				
25.	The resources that are available meet my curriculum and academic standards. They are current and up-to-date.				
26.	I recommended resources in our parent library to parents.				

27. In what areas (if any) do you wish the school library could provide more resources?

28. What are the stumbling blocks in accessing the available online tools?

29. What additional resources do you need to meet school improvement goals?

General Information

		1	2	3	4
30.	The library facility is available for my use when needed.				
31.	The library support staff is efficient in responding to your needs.				
32.	The library check out/in procedures are efficient and effective?				

33. What is the most useful part of the school library program?

34. What services do you wish the school library program offered that aren't currently available?

35. List the way(s) you think the school library program could be improved to better serve students and staff.

36. What areas would you like more staff development in the areas of library or technology?

37. Other comments/concerns/or thoughts?

Figure 8.1   Continued

Primary Age Survey

	YES	Not Sure	NO
1. Do you like coming to the school library?	☺	😐	☹
2. When you come to the school library, do you learn new things?	☺	😐	☹
3. When you come to the school library, can you get answers to your questions?	☺	😐	☹
4. When you come to the school library, do you learn how to find information?	☺	😐	☹
5. Can you find books you want to read in our school library?	☺	😐	☹
6. Can you find books to answer your questions in our school library?	☺	😐	☹
7. Do you use the school library webpage?	☺	😐	☹

8. What do you like best about the school library?

9. If you could change one thing about our school library, what would it be?

Intermediate Age Survey—Answer the following questions. Please give examples to prove your answer.

1. What are the things in our school library that make you want to come here to study, learn, read, use technology, and socialize?

2. When you come to the school library who or what helps you most as you search for answers to your questions?

3. When you come to the school library, which types of technology and software are most helpful as you try to find information?

4. What types and subjects of books would you like to find more of in our school library?

5. What other technologies would you find helpful as you seek answers to your questions in our school library?

6. What are the most helpful features of the school library webpage? Which do you use most?

7. What do you like best about the school library?

8. If you could change one thing about our school library, what would it be?

Figure 8.2 Sample Student Survey.

checkout limit is much higher than any other school in the district. The principal is also interested in the leveled library (a leveled book room of class sets—see ideas in Chapter 10). The school librarian makes sure to include these two data points in every monthly report focusing on telling the story of how the school library program is helping to support these programs.

Rationale for Data Collection

The main reason to collect data is to determine how to best help students learn. To that end, the data collected is important because it helps tell the story of the school library and provides directions on how the program can get even better for the students next year. Both are valid reasons for spending time analyzing data but each might require different kinds of data to help accomplish the goal.

Keeping track of the grade levels and teachers who work with the school librarian can be important so that the school librarian can meet with a teacher whose participation is lower than in the past. Noting a drop off in participation, the school librarian can go and talk with the teacher and get him or her collaborating once again in the library. Examining circulation statistics and seeing a drop or a gain can help determine what might need to be done in the library to bring students in to check out or deciding what has been working well so one can continue to see the circulation grow.

Additional questions one might ask is standardized test scores. How does what happen in the school library impact those scores? There needs to be data and evidence to prove to administrators the strong link between the two. This isn't easy when the test doesn't necessarily have a whole section that focuses on the instruction of the library. Instead, the librarian and classroom teacher have to look at their collaborative projects, determine what they taught, and how that might have been assessed in the standardized test. It isn't a definitive answer, but it is a start to the conversation of the libraries' impact.

Sharing the Results

Not only is it important to collect and analyze data to help the school librarian make the program even better it is also important to use that data to help tell the school librarian's story to others. Chapter 3 provides a variety of communication methods for sharing the good news with various stakeholders. Data is an important way to help tell the story of the effective school library.

Modesty has gone out of style. School librarians need to be sharing all the great things they are doing with their teachers, administrators, parents, and students. All the stakeholders need to know the great things happening in that school library so they can tell others.

Long-Term Planning

Long-term planning is important for two reasons. (A) It forces an assessment of where the program is now and (B) creates a roadmap of where the program needs to go. The long-term plan is how to get from A to B. This would be part of the role of the library advisory committee.

Having input from various stakeholders builds a stronger plan and it creates people vested in helping the school library program get from A to B. Long-term plans can focus on the entire school library program or can be compartmentalized to special areas or parts.

Long-term plans should be for three to five years. Aligning the plans to the school improvement plan is critical. How can the school library program impact student success? The plan should address those elements. The plan will encompass the entire program—instruction, collections, budgets, technology, and so forth. All the elements overlap to create a successful program and that starts with a successful plan.

The school librarian should not create plans. Administrators, teachers, students (if possible) should all have inputs in creating a long-term plan for the school library. The librarian, acting as a facilitator, can provide resources and research to help design the course. The road map, if created with stakeholders, can help in the implementation because they already have the buy in as they helped create the plan.

Instruction

Creating long-term lesson plans or a curriculum map of the school library program's instruction is very helpful in planning the big picture of when different classes will be working on different skills and units. The curriculum map creates a visual to help with the collection development as discussed earlier in this chapter.

In Figure 4.5, there is a sample of a yearlong plan/curriculum map for the school library program. With this map, the school librarian can determine which grade levels or specific teachers he or she need to target. He or she can also look at where there may be gaps in instruction. The instruction plan should be in a constant state of flex. As standards change, as the needs of students change, and as technology changes, the plan should be able to be altered and adapted.

Collections

School library collections are a great example of how a systematic long-term plan is helpful. Having a plan on how to keep the collection current and improve it can be instrumental in getting additional funding dollars. Library automation software collects statistics and data about the collection. Most systems will tell the average copyright dates for each section.

Use curriculum mapping to determine what areas in the collection are most critical to the curriculum taught in the school. While school library collections strive to cover a wide range of topics like the public library, school library collections are much more driven by curriculum, so the collection should reflect that. Also gain input from the teachers and students. While the collection may have sufficient resources on a topic, are there a variety of reading levels available to meet all the students' needs? Are there sufficient materials to meet students' recreational reading needs? Input from others will be another data point in helping to determine the plan. Are there sufficient resources that students and teachers need based on the school improvement plan and building goals? Student wants and interests?

An effective long-term plan addresses more than just print resources. The school librarian needs to assess the electronic resources as well. What databases does the library have available? What new resources might be there? Is the budget able to add new resources or should the school librarian substitute new things for resources not being used? These factors should be taken into account while deciding what resources need to be purchased. It may make more sense to subscribe to online databases than to add additional print resources on a topic.

Technology

Technology is another area where long-term planning is a must. Attending any of the technology conferences, one can quickly see that the availability of technology focused on education is massive. There are countless gadgets, tools, software, and pieces of equipment ready for purchasing. As with building the collection, there should be some sort of systematic approach to purchasing technology.

The degree of influence the school librarian has on spending technology dollars varies by school district. In some districts, all those decisions are made at the district level. In other districts, those decisions are made at the building level. The school librarian's role in district and building leadership with technology is important. School librarians can be a model and a valuable resource as decisions are made. Getting involved on the planning committees at both the district and building level can be critical to demonstrate the leadership role of the school librarian. Regardless of the level at which the decisions are made, it is a good idea to know what the long-term program is in order to advocate for them.

Just like the collections in the library, technology tools are important for students. Looking at standards, there is no way to avoid students being engrossed in using these online resources. With so many choices, it is also important to make careful and deliberate decisions on what tools are the highest priorities. As more and more resources become available online (free or subscription), selection of these tools increases in importance.

Last, predicting what technology is coming will help guide which professional development is needed in the building. As school librarians have a key role in providing professional development, it is important that there is a plan in place for how to help teachers learn these new tools.

Work with the administrator and library advisory committee to determine needs and desires. Share these with administrators and district technology staff to see what might be possible. The school librarian can be the critical link between the technology department, administration, and teachers.

The library advisory committee will think about all these areas. They may go back and survey teachers, students, and parents. They may want input from central office about future plans for the district. They may want to review any data collected by the school librarian (circulation, instruction, etc.).

Once they see the data, it is time to determine the plan. Along with the school librarian, the library advisory committee can look at the data and help determine priorities. Which area needs the most work? Which areas can wait a little while? Which areas are in good shape? Make a plan on what needs to be done to help strengthen those areas that are lacking. Be sure to create estimates of what funds will be needed as well.

The last step is to match funding with needs. Quite likely the funding will not be enough to cover all the things needed. The plan puts out on the radar what the school library program needs. Principals, who are part of the library advisory committee, will know that if additional funds become available exactly how they would impact the school library program. The school librarian knows that they can also begin looking out for other funding sources as well. In times of tough finances, a multiple approach to funding will be important.

Personnel Evaluation
School Librarian

Each district has its own method for evaluating teachers. In some places, the evaluation method and tool are different for the school librarian than the classroom teacher, while in other places the form is exactly the same. Each system has its pluses and minuses.

Some states have modified the teacher evaluation form to be more specific to school librarians. This separate form takes into consideration that there are many elements outside the job of a classroom teacher that a school librarian does. On the positive side, this points out that school librarians are different but this can also be a negative if the instructional part of the school librarians' role becomes less important to evaluate. Schools are about instruction. One could argue that the job of an elementary teacher versus a high school teacher is very different. Each has his or her own "added" duties that make them unique, but yet at the same time they are evaluated on the same rubric. Why would school librarian be any different?

Other districts evaluate the school librarian on the teacher rubric. This rubric may have some items that don't apply to the school librarian, but overall much of the focus on teaching and learning is important for both school librarians and classroom teachers. At the same time an astute administrator should be able to observe what a school librarian does and assess those outside duties as they apply. School librarian should also be making sure their administrators are aware of the various roles and tasks they complete. Between the two of them it is possible to make the teacher rubric workable.

Whether in a district with one form for all or a special form for the school librarian, the important piece is the education of the administrator. What do they know about school libraries? What do they know about what a school librarian does? What do they know about school librarian and teacher collaboration? Often the school librarian needs to educate the administrators on the potential, so when they are observed they can see it. Whatever the tool, the school librarian needs to keep the lines of communication open and conversational if and when things might need some additional explanation.

One example of a potential evaluation tool for school librarians can be found on the AASL website, http://www.ala.org/aasl/sites/ala.org.aasl/files/content/guidelinesandstandards/learning4life/resources/LMS-DANIELSON.pdf. Individual states have also tackled creating an evaluation tool such as the one used in Indiana, http://www.ilfonline.org/resource/resmgr/aisle/nov_2012_school_librarian_ev.pdf, or this one from Mississippi, http://www.mde.k12.ms.us/docs/teacher-center/librarian-evaluation-appraisal-rubric-form-l2.pdf?sfvrsn=2.

Library Assistants/Clerks

If you have a library assistant, it is important that there is a formal evaluation each year. Many districts will require this as part of their employment. Likely it falls under the principal's responsibility, but often it includes input from the school librarian (and if it doesn't, it should).

It is important that the evaluation is yearly; however, if there are issues or concerns, make sure to bring them up at the time they arise instead of waiting until the evaluation. Make sure to include the administrator or whoever does the evaluation of the assistant in these conversations. If there are issues or concerns, make sure to document them. Just in case you need evidence to prove the position.

The ability to work, as a team, is so important and a library assistant can be critical to the success of the school library program. They take on many of the clerical tasks that frees up the librarian to be available for students and staff. The working relationship is the key so the library assistant sees their opinions matter and the school librarian is happy with the additional help.

Volunteers

While volunteers are not employees, it is still important to evaluate them—especially when it comes to figuring out what tasks they are comfortable with and able to complete. Some volunteers are going to be great shelvers, some are going to be great at displays and promotion, and still others will be helpful in working with students and circulation. It is important that the librarian has a clear understanding of where the right fit is for each volunteer. Sometimes it takes trying and evaluating their work to determine the right place.

In addition, if volunteers are working at the circulation desk, it will be important to provide training about student privacy and the automation system. It will be important to know that they are complying with that training. So from time to time, the librarian will want to observe those interactions.

While the volunteer isn't going to be given a formal written evaluation, it is still important for the school librarian (or library assistant) to keep on top of what the volunteers are doing and how well they are doing it.

Student Workers

If you use students as library helpers, it will be important to also have a clear grasp on their success. If they are shelving or straightening shelves, the school librarian should take time to go back and check over them from time to time.

One librarian has a test that her student workers take before they begin to be sure they have clearly understood their responsibilities. Her shelvers practice until she can decide which ones will work best in fiction or nonfiction. The evaluation helps to make sure she puts the right student with the right position.

If they are helping with technology projects, check in with the teachers they were helping. Everyone needs reaffirmation that they are doing well, so make sure to reward those students who are doing their job. For those students who are not being successful, it is time to reevaluate and find another place where they can be of help.

Works Cited

American Association of School Librarians. *Empowering Learners: Guidelines for School Library Programs.* Chicago, IL: American Association of School Librarians, 2007.

American Association of School Librarians. *Standards for the 21st Century Learner.* Chicago, IL: American Association of School Librarians, 2007.

Martin, Ann M. *Seven Steps to an Award-Winning School Library Program*, 2nd edition. Santa Barbara, CA: Libraries Unlimited, 2012.

Further Reading

"AASL Planning Guide for Empowering Learners," Accessed April 27, 2016. http://www.ala.org/aasl/standards/planning.

Andrews, Sandra D. *The Power of Data: An Introduction to Using Local, State, and National Data to Support School Library Programs.* Chicago, IL: American Association of School Librarians, 2012.

Bush, Gail, and Jami Biles Jones, eds. *Tales Out of the School Library: Developing Professional Dispositions.* Santa Barbara, CA: Libraries Unlimited, 2009.

Crowley, John D. *Developing a Vision: Strategic Planning for the Teacher Librarian in the 21st Century*, 2nd edition. Santa Barbara, CA: Libraries Unlimited, 2011.

Martin, Ann M. *Seven Steps to an Award-Winning School Library Program*, 2nd edition. Santa Barbara, CA: ABC-CLIO, 2012.

Owen, Patricia. *A 21st-Century Approach to School Librarian Evaluation.* Chicago, IL: American Association of School Librarians, 2012.

Sykes, Judith A. *Conducting Action Research to Evaluate Your School Library.* Santa Barbara, CA: Libraries Unlimited, 2013.

CHAPTER 9

Budget

Every little bit of funding inches you forward toward your ideal program.

— Cynthia Anderson and Kathi Knop, *Write Grants, Get Money*

Money—if only there was an endless supply of it available to support school library programs. Jokingly, one school librarian shared with his principal that he needed a sign to hang in the principal's office that said, "All Money Goes to the Library!" But the reality is, wouldn't that be wonderful! School librarians look for every opportunity to increase the resources at their disposal. How does the school librarian show the money spent on the library is a good return on investment? How does the school librarian create outstanding programs on limited funds? No easy answers exist to either of these questions, but they are the ones that continue to be an issue in the 21st century.

The most important thing to keep in mind is to make sure to put the learner first! How will spending these dollars help students? How will requesting that piece of equipment make an impact for student learning? What opportunities will open up for students by having this fund-raiser? Putting that in the front of the thought process helps to create a motivation and a purpose in dealing with figuring out money and budgets.

Library Funding in the 21st Century

The Every Student Succeeds Act that was passed in 2016 gives school libraries its first glimpse of potential federal funding in decades. Previously, district had not budgeted resources for libraries because of the federal funding from the 1960s and as that dried up, there were no resources available to funnel back to libraries (Dickinson 2003, p. 21).

Each state (and each district and sometimes each school) sets up its own various ways to account for the money allocated to the school library program. Some states set specific minimums per child that must be spent, while others allow each district to determine how much money they spend. Some building level administrators determine the budgets for their schools, so they can wheel huge power over the school library program. Some budgets are determined on a per pupil expenditure, while some give a flat rate to each school library, and still others are a combination. Unfortunately, in many places there is no budget for materials.

Budgeting in the 21st Century

The AASL program standards say that the school library programs should be sufficiently funded so that the library meets its goals, mission, and priorities. The guidelines recommend making a budget based off the long-term (or strategic) plan and to meet regularly with administrators to discuss the plan and the budget needs.

In the 1960 standards, it recommended purchasing one book for every student each year. Almost 50 years later that goal is very difficult for most libraries (Dickinson 2003, p. 86). The standards of subsequent years took out quantitative measures and focused more of qualitative measures. *Empowering Learners* is no different in that regard. The lack of specific numbers is due to it being very hard to set rules that will apply across the country. Each school has to set its own priorities and needs and the budget it needs to reach those. Specific standards can also be limiting. One may assume that if they hit that number they've reached all their school library needs when in reality they may need additional dollars due to years of neglect. This becomes another good opportunity for the library advisory committee to weigh in on the needs of the school library program. An important conversation can be started by asking, "What does our school library program need to have to help our students be successful?"

Collections continue to evolve. The onslaught of different formats, different pieces of technology are having an impact on the library budgets as well. Part of crafting the budget will be determining what new formats need to be added to the school library collection. Chapter 10 will focus on the collection, but it is important to mention that these new formats and resources need to be considered when creating the school library budget.

Budget Resources

In the annual March issue of *School Library Journal*, www.slj.com, it usually publishes the current average cost of library books. National statistics like this can be useful in determining a budget for the library. As the school librarian works to decide how many new materials he or she needs, the librarian can use this price to estimate the money he or she needs to make those new purchases.

Gail Dickinson recommends using data from the local collection to determine a budget. What was the average cost of a book that the school librarian bought last year? (Dickinson 2003, p. 106). She recommends doing the same with periodicals, audio/visual resources, and digital resources.

Factors to consider when making a budget are not only purchasing new materials but also including in the budget funds for replacing damaged or lost materials as well. Books also wear out eventually. Classics will need to be replaced from time to time. The updated covers often increase circulation of these great stories. Be prepared to replace these older books with newer copies, too.

The budget not only shows what the school library program needs but it provides an outline for when funds are allocated. It shows administrators that there are specific plans for dollars that are to be spent. School librarians will likely have to go back to their budget to make decisions about what the priorities are. If additional funding becomes available, the items eliminated from the budget can possibly still be purchased. The other thought is that they could be held over to the next year and are a starting place in creating the next budget.

Doug Johnson suggests that when working with budgets it is important to understand where the district gets its money from (Johnson 1995). Does it come from property taxes? Is it all allocated from the state? What is the budget creation process at the district level? Who makes those decisions about the budgets? Part of being prepared for budgets is researching how the process works.

Budget Justification

Do not be a librarian who gets a reputation for being whiny. Constantly begging "I need . . ." or "I don't have . . ." wears quickly on administrators. One associate superintendent for finances once remarked, "Librarians are the whiniest people I've ever met." His argument was—they always wanted more money for resources, more staff, more and more. Do not allow that perception to establish itself. Instead, let administrators see the goals and the rationales. They need to know how the more money and more staff will impact student achievement. See examples of revised statements in more student-focused language from Chapter 2.

The key to any budget in a school is how are those dollars going to directly impact students and student learning. The data provided should demonstrate how the additional funding would make a difference for students. For example, when asking for additional dollars for support staff, do not focus on the school librarian's needs and the lack of time to do administrative tasks. Do not focus on the clerical items that are not getting done. Instead, focus on the students. By having an assistant, it would free up 50 percent more of the school librarian's time to work with students and teachers on projects. By having an assistant, books that are ordered would get in the hands of students weeks sooner. By having an assistant, the school librarian could teach more classes in the library, in the classrooms, and in other parts of the school. By having an assistant, books that are returned could be checked in and put back on the shelves and available for the next class of students faster. This advice does not guarantee that the request will be granted. However, it is important to justify all expenses in terms of how they impact student learning.

Connecting the budget requests to specific curriculum projects or initiatives is important. How can the resources the school library have provide the tools students and teachers need? For example, with textbook adoption, the school library program could provide trade books to supplement the textbook (Cox 2008, p. 24). Designating part of the library budget to fund resources to support district initiatives can be a good move both for the students and for the school library program. Sometimes money is dedicated to new initiatives and if the library has a plan, they may be able to connect to some of that dedicated funding for the library.

More Money

Unfortunately, relying on dollars just from the district is not likely going to be sufficient for everything the school library program needs. School librarians need to be proactive to be scouting for other sources of dollars.

Grants

Grants are a great way to bring in funds to the school library. Local educational foundations often offer annual grants for teachers in the district. These are usually simple and easy to complete. Consider writing them with a teacher in the building. The grant could also be a way to build a collaborative connection to a classroom teacher.

Make sure to read the directions very carefully before applying for a grant. Make sure the library meets the eligibility requirements of the grant. Make sure the project meets all their guidelines. Also make note of the reporting process. Last, keep track of the deadline. Many districts require approval from the superintendent and/or school board before applying for a grant, so make sure to leave sufficient time to get their approval before the deadline. Reading all of the details of the grant is critically important in order to make good use of the grant-writing time.

Book Fairs

Book fairs have long been a source of funding for school libraries. While the school library doesn't always receive the book fair funding, a lot of school librarians are in charge of the fairs and therefore get to spend the profits. The money is usually kept in a building account and can be spent on a variety of things including books, magazines, videos, programs, and supplies. In some places, the book fair is the school library's sole source of funds. E-mail and webpages have become efficient ways to promote the fair to the school and community. Communicating to the patrons the goals for which the money will be used helps to encourage people to shop at the fair. For example, the book fair might have a goal to raise money to bring an author to visit the school. Adding other family events to the evening like science fair or pizza night is another way to bring in parents to help their young ones shop.

PTA/PTOs

PTA/PTOs are another source of funding for the school librarian. Many parent groups feel spending money on books, technology, and programs for the media center to be an excellent way to help the school. Because the school library is a place where all students benefit from dollars spent, parent groups see that as a good place to spend their dollars. PTA/PTOs create an annual budget. With the appropriate advocacy and communications, some items for the school library such as an author visit or support for a reading incentive program might become annual expenses. Other things like new books, special equipment, furniture, or technology might be something that the school librarian asks for periodically.

Consortium Purchases

Many areas have consortiums where you can band together to get discounts on supplies, materials, and books. These could be statewide or they could be just local areas, but the savings could make them worth the due membership. Check them out to see what options are in the area.

Money to fund programs will always be needed. Advocating for budgets that adequately fund the school library program is an annual task. However, school librarians will need to continue to remain creative, resourceful, and inventive to find the funds to create the program students and staff deserve.

Works Cited

American Association of School Librarians. *Empowering Learners: Guidelines for School Library Programs.* Chicago, IL: American Association of School Librarians, 2009.

Anderson, Cynthia, and Kathi Knop. *Write Grants, Get Money*, 2nd edition. Columbus, OH: Linworth Publishing, 2009.

Cox, Marge. "Tips for Budgeting." *Library Media Connection* 26, no. 4 (January 2008): 24.

Dickinson, Gail K. *Empty Pockets, Full Plates: Effective Budget Administration for School Librarians.* Columbus, OH: Linworth Publishing, 2003.

Johnson, Doug. "Budgeting for Mean Lean Times." *Multimedia Schools* 2, no. 5 (November-December 1995): 32–34, 36–37.

Young, Robyn R. "Eight Easy Steps to Maintain and Increase the School Library Budget." *Library Media Connection* 26, no. 4 (January 2008): 26.

Further Reading

Darby, Katie. "Library Makeover on the Cheap." *School Library Journal* 62, no. 3 (2016): 18.

Davis, Brooke. "Running a Library on a Shoestring Budget." *School Library Connection* 1, no. 6 (2016): 18–20.

Fullner, Sheryl Kindle. *The Shoestring Library*. Santa Barbara, CA: Linworth Publishing, 2010.

McClung, Paula. "Budget Cuts: How to Deal with Less." *School Library Monthly* 28, no. 5 (2012): 33.

Young, Jr., Terrence E., and Carl A. Harvey II. "Professional Development on a Shoestring." *School Library Monthly* 26, no. 9 (2010):18–21.

CHAPTER 10

Collections

The collection is at the core: it's at the center of everything we do as information professionals, and its development is the unique role that school librarians play within the learning community.

— Marcia Mardis, *The Collection Programs in Schools: Concepts and Practices*

Access to Information

The school library collection (both print and digital) is there to serve the needs of students and staff. The important thing to consider when deciding what resources and formats to include is to determine what information will be most helpful to students and staff and how they could best access it.

Traditional Collection

The traditional collection in an elementary school library includes picture books, chapter books, nonfiction, reference, and audiovisual books. Collections might also include a professional collection for staff. There might also be a collection of video resources and audiobooks.

Recent years have seen some shifts in the traditional collection. Cassette audio books were replace by CDs and now replaced with digital download and Playaways. The reference collection has moved to the circulating collection as most of what was once in a traditional print reference section is now available online. The video resources have moved from VHS to DVD to digital resources.

Databases and websites are now a critical resource in collection as eBooks are growing in popularity as a resource in school library collections. Graphic novels have grown in popularity in elementary collections.

Selection Procedures/Policies

It is important that there are clear selection policies and procedures. As mentioned in Chapter 7, there should be a selection policy approved by the school board for acquisition of materials. The school librarian can take those policies and create procedures.

The policies and procedures help to guide the school librarian to make purchases that meet the needs of the patrons, are unbiased, are in a variety of formats, and recommend the use of selection tools to help make decisions. It also gives the school librarians direction on the process for ordering materials, vendors to use, making the materials ready for the shelf.

The policies are most helpful should there be challenges to the materials by patrons or staff. The school board should also have an adopted policy for challenging materials. (See Figure 7.1 for some sample collection development policies.)

Ordering and Processing

When ordering materials, most vendors provide cataloging records and processing. Some offer this for free, while others charge for the service. Make sure to fill out any of the forms carefully and accurately in order to ensure that the records you get back will work. Some bigger districts may have cataloging services provided at the district level that help or take care of this step for the school librarian.

Library Organization
Dewey versus Other Methods

For many years, the standard way to organize a library was to alphabetize the chapter books and picture books by the author's last name. The nonfiction was organized using Dewey. In recent years, there has been a movement to organize the fiction by genres—genrefication.

Those who have made the move report increased circulation and patrons appreciate finding the types of books they like together in one place. Those in the other court fear that students are being limited to just a genre they like rather than expanding their choices. In addition, they worry that students won't be able to access resources in other types of libraries that follow a more traditional method. Another argument is the amount of time spent redoing the collection that could be focused on other projects and endeavors.

In addition, some have gone even farther and ditched the Dewey Decimal System and organized their nonfiction based on categories as well—many following the categories you might find in a bookstore. They also put the sports nonfiction next to the sports fiction. This unconventional approach seems to work for some and gives nightmares to other.

There isn't a definitive way to approach the topic. Each librarian seems to be doing what works best for them based on the school and district they work in. It is certainly worth a conversation and discussion and school librarians will have greatly varying opinions and thoughts.

Digital Curation

Digital curation is pulling together of online resources. Sue Kimmel defines the difference in a pathfinder from digital curation in that a pathfinder is a guide through resources, but the user is still determining his or her searches and what information they need. In digital curation, the person pulling the resources together already made some of those decisions (Dickinson and Repman 2014, p. 95).

There are many online looks for curation that work well for elementary school students. Symbaloo is very popular because of the ease of use and ability to customize and organize the page. Others to try include LiveBinders, Padlet, and Pearltrees. Who knows what other tools will be developed for use in the future. With the huge amount of information on the Internet (especially for elementary students), pulling the resources that are appropriate and readable can be most useful.

Databases/Online Resources

As mentioned in the technology chapter, there are many elementary-appropriate databases (see Figure 6.2) and online resources available. When the school librarian thinks about what to select for the collection, the important things to consider are connections to the curriculum/ standards, ease of use by elementary student, costs, and does it expand access to materials not otherwise found in the collection.

When working on deciding what to purchase, make sure to try the resources out with students and staff and get their input. Databases purchases are costly and a continuous yearly cost. So, making sure they are worth the expense and will be used is important. In addition, checking the stats of use is important when considering whether to keep or eliminate a database. However, it usually takes a few years (along with professional development and introductions to students) to get a clear picture of whether people will use it or not.

eBooks

More and more libraries are adding eBooks to their collections. It allows them to provide materials in additional formats. Many patrons enjoy reading them on their tablets and mobile devices. Most eBook sales are set up for an individual user. However, the major publishers are still trying to figure out how to sell them to libraries. Because eBooks don't ever fall apart, get lost, not returned, and so forth; libraries are not likely to buy replacement copies. So, publishers are still trying to figure out a business model. Some publishers sell copies that expire after so many circulations or after a certain time limit. Some publishers have raised their prices drastically above what it would cost an individual to purchase them. Some publishers are still selling them to libraries at a normal price, and still some publishers have come up with unlimited licenses and access to multiple users at the same time. Although the latter tends to be not the more popular selections that patrons are requesting.

There are many eBook platforms. Some publishers have their own platform that you can use to access their books, others have set up platforms for access of eBooks from all kind of publishers. See *School Library Journal*'s School EBook Market Directory, www.slj.com/resources/sljs-school-ebook-market-directory/#, for a list of eBook platforms and vendors. It is very important to read the contracts and agreements before committing. Do you own the eBooks if you drop the platform? How much are the hosting fees? Are their publishers that the platform can't get access? See Figure 10.1 for a list of things to consider about eBook platforms.

Print versus Digital in Elementary Schools

In recent years, there has been much lamenting about eBooks taking over the school library collection. However, that doesn't seem to be playing out that way currently. Certainly elementary school libraries need to invest in eBook collections, but they are not replacing the entire print collection. Publishers are still debating on the right model for eBooks, so the pricing and access of eBooks make it almost impossible to replace the print collection. In addition, there are some studies that indicate that students prefer print—especially for fiction reading. So, while eBooks are here and are a critical part, they are just one of the formats and ways to access information—not the only way.

Beyond the Books

There are many other formats and items that can be part of the library collection. Beyond the traditional book and online resources, other things you might consider like audiobooks—digital downloads, CDs, or Playaways. There are multiple ways to hear books read aloud. Puppets, LEGOS, and other creative items for students can be additional parts of the collection. The makerspace movement has added all sorts of resources to school libraries. Some are resources to be used in the school, and some can be available for check out.

One librarian worked with his or her resource teacher on a grant for students who needed additional support to help them focus in the classroom. They built teacher kits that could be checked out and available when a teacher had just that kind of student. The budget resources and the needs of the students and staff are the only limits of additional resources in the library.

Professional Collections

School libraries are there not just for students but faculty and staff. A small collection of resources that support the school initiatives and professional growth of the faculty could be helpful. The collection of eBooks, web resources, and print resources can be most helpful to staff. The main

Purpose	Why are you having eBooks?
Devices/portal	Which devices will your students be accessing these eBooks on?
Content decisions	Do your eBooks focus on recreational reading or curriculum/research or both? How many publishers work with the vendor?
Funding (long term/short term)	How will you pay for it? There is typically a subscription fee for most services.
Pricing	What is included in the annual fee?
Ownership of content	Who owns the content? If you quit the subscription, do you lose the content?
Formats	What are the formats in which a reader can access the book? There are many different formats depending on the reader that students are using. Are their multiple formats?
Number of circs	Some publishers limit the number of times you can circulate an eBook before you have to buy it again. You need to know this ahead of time before purchasing.
Number of access at a time	How many students can access a book at a time?
Enhancements	What additional features does the eBook provide? Is there media content? Are their links to additional information?
Roll out plan, professional development, and publicity!	How will you promote this to your teachers, students, and parents? What will you need to train these various groups to access the eBooks? How will you garner interest and use of the resources?

Figure 10.1 eBook Considerations.

budget priority should be the students, so it is important to keep track of usage to make sure budget dollars are used effectively. Sometimes other monies from the administration and/or the district departments may add professional items to the collection to help teachers with a new curriculum or program without impacting the libraries budget. Conversations with staff and administration can make sure those resources purchased for the professional collection and relevant and used.

Other Collections

Leveled Library Resources

Leveled libraries are huge parts of the resources available in elementary schools. These collections contain multiple copies of books grouped together by levels. Looking at these libraries as an opportunity, the school librarian can help select, organize, catalog, and manage the leveled library. Automation systems can track data about the use of the materials in that room. School librarians can make sure to track all the resources funneled into the leveled library. By being part of the solution in helping create these leveled libraries, school librarians can demonstrate how that room serves a purpose different than the school libraries. School libraries need to remain free choice and unleveled, and by being part of the solution of creating a leveled library, school librarians can help keep it that way (Harvey 2006).

Textbooks

Textbooks are another resource that will see dramatic change during the 21st century. Currently the print model dominates, but the publishers are offering more and more options for electronic textbooks for students. Whether it is a CD, online, or a print volume, the automation systems can also help districts track their textbooks. Destiny™ by Follett, for example, has a complete module designed to help districts track textbooks. While this may seem like something the school librarian should avoid because it is just one more thing to do, keep in mind that school librarians are the experts in keeping track of resources. There is some logic in the thought that they would be part of keeping track of textbooks as well. Being part of the solution can be important when it comes to the school library program needing things, too (Harvey 2008).

Digital textbooks are going to become more and more important as schools move to 1:1 environment. Tracking the digital content may also end up falling under the auspices of the school librarian. Certainly it is possible the devices might also. Consider how the tools at the disposal of the librarian can be helpful to such an endeavor. It might often be that school librarians want to avoid some of these tasks dealing with textbooks, but it could be a win-win for the district and some good PR for the library, too.

Equipment and/or Technology

As discussed in Chapters 6 and 8, equipment and technology purchases are not always something at the discretion of the school librarian. However, it is important that school librarians be aware of what type of resources are there and be ready to offer advice and advocate for those resources a school library (and the entire school) needs to have.

Weeding

Weeding the collection is vitally important. Outdated and worn materials make the library unappealing to students. In addition, they can be filled with misinformation. Take time to set up a system to periodically weed the collection to eliminate those resources that are old and outdated. Make sure to follow district policies for discarding the weeded materials.

One method commonly used in libraries it the CREW method. The Texas State Library publishes this guidelines and methods for weeding the collection. It can be accessed online at www.tsl.texas.gov/ld/pubs/crew/index.html. There are other systems to use when weeding, but the main focus is to have a plan and some strategies for tackling the collection systematically.

Often people wonder about weeding. What if all the books meet the criteria? What if the shelves look empty? There isn't money to replace everything. Those may all be true questions to consider, but no one is likely to increase the budget if the shelves look full. No one is going to increase the budget if no one is utilizing the old resources. Weeding can be a difficult thing to do, but in order to make sure students have access only to good resources, it is important as well.

Interlibrary Loan (ILL)

ILL is an important way to increase the collection. If the school district has several elementary schools, it is easy to share resources between the buildings. A school district pony system that travels from building to building can help move the resources are needed from one or the other. Many library automation systems can set up the ILL through their system to track requests and items sent and when they are due.

This is also a great opportunity to utilize the public library. One school district's pony system stopped by the public library once a week and allowed the schools to check out materials to expand the collection. There may be other opportunities for interlibrary around the state or country depending on the library systems in the area. Utilize them when students need materials that might be difficult to get or if budget funds make it impossible.

Children's Literature and Technology

The world of technology allows us to connect and stay current with authors or illustrators and their work. Many of them are at Twitter where you can easily follow them to learn tidbits about their latest publications and work. Podcast's such as Matthew Winners All the Wonders are great places to meet authors and illustrators. Travis Jonker and Colby Sharp have an online news program called The Yarn where they unravel the details about one book at a time. Many of the review journals like SLJ and Horn Book have their own e-mail list they send out with stories and information about books. There are several blogs that feature new and upcoming children's literature. There are many online resources like Reviews+ from ABC-CLIO's *School Library Connection* or TeachingBooks.net. While these are accessed via subscription, they can be valuable resources for the school librarian.

Collection development in the 21s century will require school librarians to think about the new formats and sources students will need to find information. Appendix A contains a list of some of the most common library vendors. These resources provided by the school library program for students and staff will be important to prepare them for the 21st century.

Works Cited

Dickinson, Gail K., and Judi Repman, eds. *School Library Management*. Santa Barbara, CA: Linworth Publishing, 2014.

Harvey, Carl A., II. "Leveling for Leverage," *Library Media Connection* 24, no. 4 (January 2006): 42.

Harvey, Carl A., II. "Textbooks: Friend or Foe," *Library Media Connection* 26, no. 4 (January 2008): 52.

Further Reading

Adams, Helen R. *Ensuring Intellectual Freedom and Access to Information in the School Library Media Program*. Santa Barbara, CA: Libraries Unlimited, 2008.

Adams, Helen R. *Protecting Intellectual Freedom and Privacy in Your School Library*. Santa Barbara, CA: Libraries Unlimited, 2013.

Cavanaugh, Terence W. *EBooks for Elementary School*. Santa Barbara, CA: Libraries Unlimited, 2014.

"Dewey or Don't We." *Knowledge Quest* 42, no. 2 (2013): 1.

Kimmel, Sue C. *Developing Collections to Empower Learners*. Chicago, IL: American Association of School Librarians, 2014.

Leverkus, Cathy, and Shannon Acedo. *Ebooks and the School Library Program: A Practical Guide for the School Librarian*. Chicago, IL: American Association of School Librarians, 2013.

Mardis, Marcia A. *The Collection Program in Schools: Concepts and Practices*. Santa Barbara, CA: Libraries Unlimited, 2016.

Scales, Pat R. *Protecting Intellectual Freedom in Your School Library: Scenarios from the Front Lines*. Chicago, IL: American Library Association, 2009.

Sheehan, Kate. *The EBook Revolution: A Primer for Librarians on the Front Lines*. Santa Barbara, CA: Libraries Unlimited, 2013.

Winner, Matthew C. "Keeping Up with Children's Literature." *School Library Connection* 1, no. 7 (2016): 19–21.

CHAPTER 11

Advocacy, Public Relations, and Marketing

Becoming influential in a school takes time, hard work, tons of patience and people skills, and a fervent desire to lead and improve a situation.

— Debra Kachel, Margaux DelGuidice, and Rose Luna, *Activism and the School Librarian: Tools for Advocacy and Survival*

Defining Advocacy, Public Relations, and Marketing

Because of the loss of positions and cuts in library budgets, it has become even more urgent for school librarians to work on public relations and advocacy. Advocacy efforts often begin too late. Once it is announced that positions may be cut or eliminated, often there is little to be done to save them. The work with public relations and advocacy must become a constant part of the school library program.

Advocacy is when someone other than the school librarian shares the message and fights for the school library program (AASL 2009). Advocacy is getting parents, students, staff, and community members to know and understand the importance of the school library program and be willing to go to bat for it. These are the people who school boards and administrators will listen to when making decisions. When school librarians speak, it often is seen as self-serving, but when a parent talks about the value of the program, they are perceived as speaking with sincerity and a real-life story.

Public relations is all the work the school librarian does to share what is happening in the school library, why it is important, and how it connects to the curriculum This communication is one way—from the school librarian to the stakeholders (AASL 2009). This can be done via newsletters, e-mails, face-to-face conversations, students sharing at home what they did at school that day, and articles in the newspaper. Tools such as blogs and wikis are ways to share with parents and students the happenings in the school library.

Marketing is developing a plan of what customers need and how can the school library program provide those services (AASL 2009). This dovetails perfectly into the long-term plans discussed in Chapter 7. The school librarian uses public relations to promote the services outlined in the plan and then when patrons are getting the services they need, in turn, will create advocates for the school library program.

Advocates

School libraries are often first on the list to be eliminated during tough financial times. Once the positions are gone, it is difficult to get them back. By building advocates, the school librarian creates a group of people who are willing to go to bat in for those difficult times by advocating that eliminating or cutting school libraries is not the answer to the budget problems. It creates a network of people who are sharing what is happening in the school library program in the community, so that perhaps the discussion of cuts will never come up.

Building Advocates

Creating advocates for the school library is building partnerships. Partnerships with principals, parents, and students are crucial so that they see why the school library is important. For administrators, it might be how the school library program plays a critical role in achieving the school improvement goals. For parents it might be how the school library program provides critical resources and support for helping their child learn to read and develop into lifelong learners. For students it might be the support they receive from the school librarian during a research project or guidance on finding the perfect book. Connecting the goals of the school library program to the goals of the stakeholders is the link that helps in building advocates.

Do not expect that just by doing the job (and doing it well) advocates will instantly appear. Doing a great job is only the first step. Creating advocates also requires educating them on why the school library program is critical. They need to see examples. Show them:

✦ How the school library program contributes to the school improvement plan.

✦ How the school library program circulation statistics show a connection to improving students reading skills.

✦ How what happens in the school library impacts standardized test scores.

✦ How the collaboration log demonstrates that the 21st century skills are embedded into instruction.

Never assume that someone "gets it" by just watching. Take time to talk with the advocates and show them the data to support the school library program being a critical element in the school.

Promotion

School librarians tend to be quiet. No, not that stereotypical "shhh"er, but rather they do not tend to share the great things happening in their school library. School librarians need to be telling the story of what is happening in the school library program. Share the great student accomplishments and how they are important to the school.

Some adults have no memory of an elementary school library. Some schools might have just had a few shelves in the back of the classroom that every nine weeks the custodians rotated among the four elementary buildings so there was a new selection of books to choose from. A lot of the books were from the 1950s, 1960s, and 1970s and had been rebound at least once. Others may remember the cranky old lady who quickly checked out the books to the students to get them out of the library. She may have been called the librarian even if she wasn't a trained professional. If those are all the memories someone has about the library, how can he or she ever begin to conceptualize its importance? The answer can be simple. Today's school librarian needs to paint a new positive image for them of what the library can do.

This is a very common situation for school library programs. While there has been a huge evolution in what the school library programs do and the role the school librarian plays, the perception some people have of school libraries has not changed. The school librarian needs to be in the forefront showing people the school library program of the 21st century.

Some may think that promoting the school library program takes up valuable time when they could be working with students or teachers, but the time is well spent when those students, teachers, and administrators begin to understand what the school library program is all about.

Designing Promotions

Chapter 3 provided a plethora of resources used to communicate with stakeholders. Take advantage of those communication vehicles. They can be very powerful in sharing the message about the school library. In reality, almost anything the school librarian does can be an opportunity to promote the school library program.

Invite teachers to see the new resources that have just arrived. Mingle among them and point out books that might be helpful to them. Talk about ideas of possible projects based on the books. Following the teacher preview, leave the books out so students can begin checking them out. Highlight some of the new formats of materials at a staff meeting. Share a new online tool periodically. Introduce at a staff meeting, follow-up with e-mail, and then visit their professional learning community (PLC) time to offer individual support.

Bringing authors to schools is an exciting way to engage students in the love of reading and writing. It creates a memory for students, which they will cherish long after they leave the doors of the school. When inviting an author to visit the school, put together a simple invitation. Send it to every central office administrator and the school board members. This gives them a glimpse into the special events happening in school library. In addition, the school librarians collaborate each year to create a packet of projects and resources to share with the teachers about the visiting author, too. The packet shows them how it connects to what they are teaching in the classroom. Invite parents to come and see the author presentations. Because while an author visit might just be a one-time deal, if the students, teachers, and parents get excited about the event, the PTO just might set up an annual line item in their budget.

Invite administrators to the school library, so they can see the work students are doing. Encourage them to talk to students about what they are learning. Highlight projects in the school library newsletter and blog, so that teachers can be recognized for collaborating with the school librarian. Take pictures of events, lessons, projects, speakers, and so forth. These can be used in newsletters, on the web, parts of presentations, and blogs. Have students record a week in review podcast that students and parents can listen to over the Internet.

Simple stats about the library can turn into public relations elements, too. For example, one school librarian added up all the grants he had received in the past five years. Some of these directly benefited the library and others were written to help with resources in the school such as the leveled library. When the tally was done, it added up to over $50,000, therefore, the school librarian sent off a quick e-mail to the principal. The principal was so impressed that he put it in the next school newsletter about how much money had been raised because of the school library program.

Marketing Plan

Marketing the school library program goes hand in hand with the long-term plans discussed in Chapter 8. Another element of long-term planning is doing research to determine the needs of the users. This is a critical step in long-term planning. While the school library program is based on what students need to learn, at the same time it needs to be responsive to the recreational needs of student. The formats of materials, the types of resources, the types of recreational reading, and the layout of the facility are all elements that can control how inviting the school library is and how much the users come to the school library. It is another data point that will be helpful in designing a long-term plan to move the library forward.

Legislation—ESSA

One of the biggest legislative victories for school libraries in recent years is the inclusion of school libraries in the Every Student Succeeds Act (ESSA). The newest education law has many opportunities for school librarians. Check out some of the resources and keep abreast as the opportunities arise:

✦ American Association of School Librarians—http://www.ala.org/aasl/advocacy/legislation/essa

✦ School Library Advocacy—http://www.schoollibraryadvocacy.org/

At this point, the process is just beginning. Keep in touch with the state professional school library organization and AASL on the latest. Be ready to take advantage of the opportunities for funding should they come the way of the school library. There will be need for continued advocacy in this arena and with getting school libraries' share of the funding with this law.

Resources

The American Association of School Librarians provides a wealth of resources to support advocacy efforts at the local level. The Advocacy Toolkit, www.ala.org/ala/mgrps/divs/aasl/aaslissues/toolkits/aasladvocacy.cfm, provides resources to develop a public awareness campaign for the school library. The School Library Health and Wellness toolkit, www.ala.org/ala/mgrps/divs/aasl/aaslissues/toolkits/slmhealthandwellness.cfm, is designed to help being proactive in garnering supporters for the school library. The time to be prepared is long before any thoughts of cuts are thought about. The final kit provides resources for when the budget ax is just about to fall. The Crisis Toolkit, www.ala.org/ala/mgrps/divs/aasl/aaslissues/toolkits/crisis.cfm, is there to help when positions or budgets are being cut.

Advocates promote and support school library programs. Every program needs to ensure they have a strong contingency of advocates who are there in good times and bad. Waiting until the damage is done is too late. Advocacy requires people to be proactive! Success will be achieved when no one would even think of eliminating or cutting school library programs.

Work Cited

"Definitions of Advocacy, PR, Marketing." *American Association of School Librarians.* Accessed May 9, 2009. http://www.ala.org/ala/mgrps/divs/aasl/aaslissues/aasladvocacy/definitions.cfm.

Further Reading

AASL Educators of School Librarians Section. *Preservice Toolkit.* American Association of School Librarians, 2016. Accessed April 19, 2016. http://www.ala.org/aasl/sites/ala.org.aasl/files/content/aaslissues/toolkits/PreserviceEducators_Toolkit_FINAL_2016-03-17.pdf.

Anderson, Mary Alice. "Leadership: What Makes Us Tick?," *Library Media Connection* 24, no. 6 (March 2006): 14.

Church, Audrey P. *Tapping into the Skills of 21st-Century School Librarians: A Concise Handbook for Administrators.* Lanham, MD: Rowman & Littlefield Education, 2015.

Levitov, Deborah D., ed. *Activism and the School Librarian: Tools for Advocacy and Survival.* Santa Barbara, CA: Libraries Unlimited, 2012.

Morris, Rebecca J. *School Libraries and Student Learning: A Guide for School Leaders.* Cambridge, MA: Harvard Educational Publishing Group, 2015.

"School Library Advocacy." SchoolLibraryAdvocacy.org. Accessed April 27, 2016. http://www.schoollibraryadvocacy.org/.

CHAPTER 12

Opportunities for leadership for the school librarian are many. School librarians have to take the initiative when it comes to becoming a leader in their school and in school improvement, because those will be critical elements in creating successful and thriving school library programs.

— Carl A. Harvey II, *No School Library Left Behind: Leadership, School Improvement, and the Media Specialist*

Allison Zmuda and Violet Harada in their book Librarians as Learning Specialists argue that school librarians have to take responsibility for the learning that happens in the school library and demand that the quality of instruction meets high standards. Teachers often want to come in to do a very low-level fact and find project. School librarians have to be willing to help that teacher see other opportunities that would be more meaningful for the students. School librarian has to move beyond just the perception of that person who deals with books, but rather be seen as a curriculum leader with a wealth of resources and ideas ready to implement.

School librarians have to reach beyond the library and be active participants in the school, which in turn will help the school library program grow. Volunteer to serve on building committees such as the influential school improvement committee. Be aware of new initiatives and school-wide campaigns, and then articulate how the school library program can support and enhance those initiatives. Recently on a listserv, a school librarian posted about a new initiative happening in the school and he wondered if any school librarian had been a part of it. Several of the replies said they had tried to stay clear of the curricular initiative, as they didn't see how it impacted the school library program. Taking a head-in-the-sand approach leaves the school library program out of the loop and can relegate it to being deemed unimportant. The school library program has the potential to be a great influence on almost any initiative in the school. It is important to take the lead and be part of the conversation.

Consider the school that was designing a new behavior plan model. The emotional disability teacher was leading the planning and was given a release day to work on it. She asked the school librarian to help because she knew he had a global perspective of the school, access to finding resources, and technology skills. Strong advocacy for the program and consistent collaboration with colleagues will build opportunities for the school librarian to influence what happens in the school.

The school library profession can be one of isolation. Often schools are staffed with only one school librarian, so there is no one else who can relate to the job the school librarian does. Professional organizations and resources provide connections to those who understand. Networking with colleagues face to face at conferences and virtually through tools such as LM_Net, Twitter, and blogs are an important part of how the school librarian can connect with others and grow. The old adages of "I don't have time to learn about a _____. (blog, Twitter, Facebook, wiki, listserv, etc.)" or "I can't be away from my library" are positions that are contrary to professional growth. The reality is a school librarian cannot be successful in the 21st century without building these contacts and using these tools. School librarians must be lifelong learners just like the students!

School Librarian
Professional Organizations

Long ago it was just an expectation that everyone joined the professional organization associated with his or her career. In today's world, that does not seem to be the case. If one is around the AASL Affiliate Assembly, he or she often hears that many state organizations have seen a decline in membership in recent years. However, school librarians who do not belong to their state and national organization have no idea what they are missing. Professional organizations should be a part of any personal learning network. The resources, the networking, the advocacy, the conferences, and the sense of belonging are essential in creating a 21st-century school library.

It is an investment to belong to a professional organization, but one has to be a member to have a voice in the organization. Even if one can't attend the conferences, there are still opportunities for virtual participation on committees. One doesn't have the right to complain about what his or her state or national organization does or doesn't do if he or she isn't a member. They have the opportunity to voice their opinions and thoughts as a member. Many organizations are tapping into these online tools such as blogs, wikis, and webinars to connect with folks all over the state and country.

Professional organizations are advocating for school librarians, so more the members, the stronger the organization's voice. The contacts that one makes through a professional organization become a network of colleagues to call on when advice and counsel is needed. When attending a national (or state) conference for the first time, one gets the opportunity to listen and meet those folks who are leading the profession. Not only does one find out they are just ordinary people but it also becomes a two-way learning adventure because they want to learn just as much from you as you want to learn from them.

AASL standards are an investment in the future of the field and students. There are costs associated with creating and writing these standards, and the professional association has to fund those costs. These are major undertakings that the professional organization does for the entire library community. Being a member helps to support the organization that is leading in defining what the profession will look like in the years ahead.

Last, there is much to be said for giving back to a profession. It is important to belong, to be an active member, and to serve on committees. Being active in the profession gives one the ability to help make the profession even better. Each year when the renewal form for membership arrives in the mailbox (or e-mail inbox), think about how belonging helps improve school libraries across the state and country. Don't miss out on a minute of the opportunities that lie ahead in the coming year. The return on the investment is way more than the dollars spent. So, join now!

Professional Development

The traditional forms of professional development such as conferences, workshops, and classes are all available and certainly viable opportunities for learning.

The AASL hosts a national conference every two years. This is the only national conference completely dedicated to school libraries. The largest national library conferences are the American Library Association's annual conference and midwinter meetings. These two events each year are where the heart of the work for the national professional organization is done.

Beyond ALA and AASL, there are also other national conferences that may appeal to school librarians. The International Society for Technology in Education's annual conference each summer is packed with full of technology resources and uses in education. The International Literacy Association (ILA) annual conference also provides another opportunity for school librarian as it connects with the mission to develop lifelong readers. Because of the variety of roles school librarians play, there are many conferences and professional opportunities that will develop skills, build networks, and become innovators and leaders. Choosing which conferences and sessions to attend at the conference can become the hard part.

Most state library associations have their own conference each year. This is a good place for hearing what others in the state are doing. In addition, a good place for the school librarian to share some of the good things happening in their library. The connection with vendors at conference is also a great time to stay up on what new tools and resources are available.

LM_Net, http://www.lm-net.info/, has been around since the early 1990s and is one of the most active listservs in the country. Every school librarian should join and become one of the 10,000+ members. It is a forum for sharing and learning together. As collaborative technology, LM_Net has taken off in new directions with its own LM_Net wiki, lmnet.wikispaces.com, where documents, presentations, and other resources that don't work over e-mail can be posted for all to share.

There are many tools that can be used to expand a personal learning network as well, such as blogs, Twitter, and Facebook. All of these are places where school librarian can gather, interact with other school librarians (and other educators), and continue to learn and expand their knowledge on this changing information landscape. TL Café hosts a monthly webinar and TL News Night. AASL holds webinars for both members and nonmembers. Content is archived in the eCollab platform. Members have free access and others can subscribe. Many free webinars are also available on edWeb. ABC-CLIO, Follett, Mackin, and others host a variety of webinars centered around school library issues. See Figure 12.1 for potential online professional development.

Something else to ponder is staff development that happens in the school. Often school librarians are left out of the loop on some of these trainings because the person planning may think it does not apply to the school librarian. However, school librarian should be part of those trainings. Consider the example of a building that opted to implement a new assessment. Now, putting aside opinions about too many assessments, this was going to be a school-wide initiative, so the school librarian felt it was important to attend. It was never intended that the school librarian would give the assessment, but knowing what the tests were and now they were administered could be help in analyzing the data and when collaborating with teachers.

Personal Learning Networks (PLN)

In recent years, people have been developing personal learning network (PLN). These networks are full of other librarians, technologists, and educators who have easy access to learn and interact with each other. PLNs have grown out of the use of online tools to connect. Facebook, Twitter, Google+, and blogs have all built a network of opportunity for sharing and collaborating. FaceTime, Google Hangouts, and webinars are now easy to create and connect; therefore, many people have gone out on their own to create them. When you add all the people from face-to-face adventures to online adventures and put them all together this is a personal learning network. School librarians are often isolated and a PLN allows a school librarian to build their own learning network.

Writing and Presenting

Often the first response when someone suggests to a school librarian to write an article or turn in a proposal to present at a conference is "I don't do anything that special" or "I don't have time for that." School librarians are way too modest. Sharing the great things one does not only is helpful to other school librarians but it is a major learning opportunity for the school librarian as well.

Writing an article or giving a presentation is a very reflective experience. It gives the school librarian the chance to sit back and think about the project—what went well, what could go better the next time, and what did the students learn. Reflection is a critical part of the learning

AASL eCollab—access via membership or subscription
http://www.ala.org/aasl/ecollab

AASL free webinars
http://www.ala.org/aasl/ecollab/complimentary

edWeb Communities
http://home.edweb.net/

TL Café Webinars
http://tlvirtualcafe.wikispaces.com/

TL News Night
http://tlvirtualcafe.wikispaces.com/TL+News+Night

PLN Connections—Twitter, Facebook, etc.

Figure 12.1   Online Professional Development.

process and often one does not take time to do it because as soon as one project is finished the next one starts. When one writes or presents, it forces one to make time to reflect and rethink about the entire project.

Another reflective opportunity is to post periodically on a blog. The element that is added here is the ability to interact with the readers. People can comment on the reflection for a dialogue to be created and thereby improving on the project even more. Sharing provides an avenue to bring one outside of school libraries and reflect on making the school library program even better. Remember that the blog is there for all to read, so make sure that the writing is appropriate for everyone (the superintendent or school board members) to read.

Building/District Leadership
Professional Development

School librarians should be an active part of providing professional development in their buildings. They work with every teacher in the building. They are a natural to be leaders in using technology in the building. They hold a bounty of resources in the school libraries. Combine all this together and it makes logical sense that school librarian should be offering professional development to teachers.

The strength in school library programs comes from both literacy and technology. The school librarian has on his or her agenda to help teachers use technology effectively and give teachers ideas for helping their students with reading, research, and writing. Before starting, make sure to assess the staff with a survey or other instrument to determine what their needs really are. No sense rehashing things teachers already feel comfortable using. The survey also needs to take into account the school improvement goals. Any professional development that is offered should connect back to that plan.

Make sure you market the session by offering a title that applies to the school improvement plans and sounds inviting. Title the session "Using Digital Video Cameras as a Literacy Station" or "Using Digital Video Camera as a Fluency Monitor" and teachers will be interested in attending and engaged in the session. For example, one school librarian knew the focus of the building was on literacy stations. So, each month he offered a short, 30-minute session focusing on one piece of technology and how it connected to literacy.

Using technology as a training tool is also important. School librarians should model best practices. Put handouts for the workshops online or in a Google Drive folder. Also, use a digital curation tool to collect online tools and resources to share with staff. It gives the school librarian just one more way to share ideas and offer suggestions and to be seen as a leader.

Committees

Everybody wishes they could attend more meetings—ok, maybe not. But, the school librarian has an important voice that needs to be heard. When the opportunity to serve on district committees comes along, one should consider volunteering for it. Technology, English Language Learners, school improvement, textbook adoption, or whatever the committee might be, they all have a purpose in helping the district move forward. Having a school librarian on these committees provides a perspective that is important, and it is the key for people to see the school librarian as helping to work toward solutions.

The same applies for building level committees. Look at the committees that the school library program can best be of assistance such as a literacy or technology committee. In addition, be involved in those committees that make important decisions such as data analysis or school improvement team. Being active and involved in the building, in the district, and in the professional organizations will only help one be a better school librarian.

A conversation between two librarians once focused on building and district committees. One was lamenting about having to attend. She had all this stuff to do, classes to plan, and she just didn't have time. The other librarian came back with a much more important outlook. The more places the school librarians is seen, the more active the school librarian is in the school, and the more places the school library voice is heard, the more often stakeholders will understand what school libraries are all about.

Twenty-first century school librarians are leaders! Developing leadership skills is a critical component to the job. School librarians need to be helping to lead and guide the building, the district, and the profession. As leaders in the 21st century, school librarians have great potential. They have great potential for impacting student achievement. They have great potential to impact curriculum. They can have great potential to impact in professional development. They have great potential to change the perceptions of school library programs. Those are some great opportunities in the 21st century. Now school librarians need to just take advantage of them!

Works Cited

Harvey, Carl A., II. *No School Library Left Behind: Leadership, School Improvement, and the Media Specialist.* Columbus, OH: Linworth Publishing, 2008.

Zmuda, Allison and Violet H. Harada. *Librarians as Learning Specialists: Meeting the Learning Imperative for the 21st Century.* Westport, CT: Libraries Unlimited, 2008.

Further Reading

Coatney, Sharon, ed. *The Many Faces of School Library Leadership.* Santa Barbara, CA: Libraries Unlimited, 2010.

Martin, Ann M. *Empowering Leadership: Developing Behaviors for Success.* Chicago, IL: American Association of School Librarians, 2014.

Zmuda, Allison, and Violet H. Harada. *Librarians as Learning Specialists: Meeting the Learning Imperative for the 21st Century.* Westport, CT: Libraries Unlimited, 2008.

APPENDIX

This is a list of vendors in major categories related to school libraries. This is not an exhaustive list, but rather a place to get started.

Audio/Visual Resources

Books on Tape—http://www.booksontape.com/

Library Video Company—http://www.libraryvideo.com/

Recorded Books—http://www.recordedbooks.com/

eBooks

Baker & Taylor Axis 360—http://www.btol.com/axis360.cfm

Follett—http://www.follettlearning.com/books-materials/learn/digital-content/follett-ebooks/ebook-management

Mackin—https://www.mackin.com/

Overdrive–K-12—http://company.overdrive.com/education/k-12-schools/

Elementary Database

ABDO Publishing—http://abdopublishing.com/our-products/abdo-zoom

Britannica—https://www.britannica.com/

Capstone Publishing—http://www.capstonepub.com/library/

EBSCO—https://www.ebscohost.com/schools

Gale—Cengage Learning—http://www.gale.com/

Grolier Online/Book Flix—http://scholasticlibrary.digital.scholastic.com/digital/

ProQuest—http://www.proquest.com/

Rosen Publishing—https://www.rosenpublishing.com/

TeachingBooks.net—https://www.teachingbooks.net/

World Book Online—http://store.worldbook.com/

Jobbers

Baker & Taylor – http://www.btol.com

Bound to Stay Bound Books—http://www.btsb.com/

Follett Library Resource—http://www.titlewave.com/

Mackin—https://www.mackin.com/

Perma-Bound—https://www.perma-bound.com/

Rainbow Book Company—https://www.rainbowbookcompany.com/

Periodicals

EBSCO Information Services—http://www.ebsco.com

Popular Subscription Service—http://www.popularss.com/

W.T. Cox—http://www.wtcox.com/

Professional Materials

ALA Editions—http://www.alaeditions.org/

Libraries Unlimited—http://www.abc-clio.com/LibrariesUnlimited.aspx

School Library Connection—http://slc.librariesunlimited.com

School Library Journal—http://www.slj.com

Teacher Librarian—http://teacherlibrarian.com/

School Library Book Publishers

ABDO Publishing—http://abdopublishing.com/

Bearport Publishing Company, Inc.—http://bearportpublishing.com/

Capstone Publishers—http://www.capstonepub.com/library/

Cherry Lake Publishing—http://cherrylakepublishing.com/

Crabtree Publishing—http://www.crabtreebooks.com/

DK Publishing—http://www.dk.com/us/

Enslow Publishers—http://www.enslow.com/

Gareth Stevens Publishing—https://www.garethstevens.com/

Hachette Livre – http://www.hachette.com/en/

HarperCollins—https://www.harpercollins.com/

Houghton Mifflin Harcourt—http://www.hmhco.com/

Lerner Publishing Group—https://www.lernerbooks.com/Pages/Home.aspx

Norwood House Press—https://www.norwoodhousepress.com/

Penguin Random House—http://www.penguinrandomhouse.com/

Rosen Publishing—https://www.rosenpublishing.com/

Rourke Publishing—http://rourkeeducationalmedia.com/

Scholastic Library Publishing—http://scholasticlibrary.digital.scholastic.com/

Simon and Schuster—http://www.simonandschuster.com/

Toon Books—http://www.toon-books.com/

World Book—http://store.worldbook.com/

Supplies

Brodart—http://www.brodart.com

DEMCO—http://www.demco.com

The Library Store—http://www.thelibrarystore.com/

Video

Discovery Education—Streaming Plus—http://www.discoveryeducation.com/what-we-offer/streaming-plus-digital-media/

Learn360—http://support.infobaselearning.com/index.php?/videolearn360

Library Video Company—http://www.libraryvideo.com/

Safari Montage—http://www.safarimontage.com/

Weston Woods—https://westonwoods.scholastic.com